The Nationally Syndicated
Columnist and author of
Multiple Sarcasm

Alice Kahn

MY LIFE
AS A GAL

A COLLECTION

"BOLD...HOMESPUN...SCATHINGLY FUNNY...FEW
WRITERS TODAY ARE AS SENSITIVE TO THE
CATACLYSMIC CHANGES THAT HAVE COME TO
AMERICAN LIFE SINCE THE 50s."
—*San Francisco Chronicle*

WIT, WARMTH, AND WISDOM — ALICE KAHN A COLUMNIST FOR THE 90s!

MY LIFE AS A GAL . . . "Kahn has more hits per page than any of her rival feminine humorists . . . not a dumb thought or dud joke throughout."

—*Kirkus Reviews*

"Seldom is Kahn so violently and cruelly aggressive as to be termed sarcastic. She is instead satirical—employing irony, ridicule and wit to expose folly, including her own."

—*Chicago Tribune*

"Looking for a humorist whose observations are a little sharper? A little more pungent? A little more, as they say, now? . . . Kahn finds lunacy among the humdrum . . . all of it is wacko wacko funny."

—*Arizona Daily Star*

"Alice Kahn's name isn't exactly a household word, but it should be."

—*San Antonio Express News*

QUANTITY SALES

Most Dell books are available at special quantity discounts when purchased in bulk by corporations, organizations, and special-interest groups. Custom imprinting or excerpting can also be done to fit special needs. For details write: Dell Publishing, 666 Fifth Avenue, New York, NY 10103. Attn.: Special Sales Department.

INDIVIDUAL SALES

Are there any Dell books you want but cannot find in your local stores? If so, you can order them directly from us. You can get any Dell book in print. Simply include the book's title, author, and ISBN number if you have it, along with a check or money order (no cash can be accepted) for the full retail price plus $1.50 to cover shipping and handling. Mail to: Dell Readers Service, P.O. Box 5057, Des Plaines, IL 60017.

My Life as a Gal

ALICE KAHN

A DELL TRADE PAPERBACK

A DELL TRADE PAPERBACK

Published by
Dell Publishing
a division of
The Bantam Doubleday Dell Publishing Group, Inc.
666 Fifth Avenue
New York, New York 10103

Acknowledgment is made to the following magazines and publishers in whose pages
these articles first appeared:

Berkeley Monthly: "Modern Romance," August 1985; "My Neighborhood, My Self,"
December 1985.
East Bay Express: "2Good 2Be 4Gotten," June 21, 1985; "Desperately Seeking . . .
Anyone," April 5, 1985; "Ask Ms. Popsych," February 8, 1985; "Town Without
Porno," February 3, 1984; "Where Have All the Yuppies Gone?", July 26, 1985;
"Jog Is Dead," August 16, 1985; "The Momist Manifesto," October 18, 1985;
"Adventures in the Book Trade," May 31, 1985; "The End Is Near," March 8, 1985;
"Day Care Nightmares," June 29, 1984; "Heavy Traffic," April 6, 1984; "All in a
Day's Work," November 22, 1985; "California Drifting," July 19, 1985; "A Night
in the Suburbs," July 6, 1984; "Dr. Oops' Revised Sex Guide," January 31, 1986;
"Scooped," August 3, 1984; "Back-to-Schools," August 30, 1985; "The Real
Thing," October 4, 1985; "Turning Forty," February 7, 1986; "Porno-to-Go";
"Lookin' At You, Kid"; "All the Way Home"; and "She Saved the Lounging Suit"
San Francisco Chronicle: "Legacy of the Oval Bed"; "The King and I"; "Ms. Bad
Manners"; "The Saga of Honest Al"; "Another (Yawn) Orgasm"; "Professor of
Gambling"; "Beverly Hills Anything"; "Tragedy of the Single Man"; and "A
Plague of Pigeons, A Scourge of Squab"
San Francisco Focus: "What's Love Got to Do with It?"
West Magazine: "How to Raise a Perfect CHUMP," December 22, 1985; "Jerry Garcia
and the Call of the Weird," December 30, 1985

Copyright © 1987 by Alice Kahn

ISBN: 0-440-50157-1

Reprinted by arrangement with Delacorte Press.

Printed in the United States of America

Published simultaneously in Canada

November 1988

10 9 8 7 6 5 4 3 2 1

MV

PN6162
. K26
1988x

For Eddie

Contents

CONTENTS

ACKNOWLEDGMENTS

For every man there's a woman but for this gal, there've been a lot of guys. There but for the grace of John Raeside and *The East Bay Express* much of this would not have been written. Most of these pieces first appeared in the *Express*. Thanks also to Rob Hurwitt, who questioned my spelling and my good taste.

Praise be to fortune that I found the intelligent yet still enthusiastic Peter Sussman, who is now my main man, editorialwise, at the San Francisco *Chronicle*. Peter suggested such outrageous topics as "Another (Yawn) Orgasm Story" and "She Saved the Lounging Suit." Many thanks to Rosalie Wright for her support.

I am also indebted to Jeffrey Klein *(San Jose Mercury News West Magazine)* who is raising his own perfect chumps, Tracy Johnston *(Berkeley Monthly)* who led me to a California love guru, and Amy Rennert *(San Francisco Focus)* who published "What's Love Got to Do with It?"

Thanks also to my friends Toni Casal and Judy and Dobby Boe, who let me steal their best lines. Eternal gratitude to my agent, Ellen Levine, and editor, Susan Moldow, without whom *My Life as a Gal*, as we know it, would not exist. Undying love to the readers who didn't put me down. But most of all, I thank my own little Cosa Nostra—Eddie, Emma, and Hannah—for not having me rubbed out.

INTRODUCTION

The Nurse Who Knew Too Much

Everyone knows that there are three phases to a woman's life but no one has identified what they are. It's really quite simple. There is girlhood, galhood, and old girlhood. In this book, a collection of essays, memoirs, and silly thoughts, mostly published as newspaper columns in northern California, I document my passage through these phases not so much as an apologia but as a work of art. (Actually, not so much a work of art as a midlife crisis of egomaniacal proportions.) And since there's no use crying over old girlhood, why not exploit my psychological problems for fun and profit? (Not so much a midlife crisis as an exercise in indecent exposure.)

Girlhood (described here in "Back-to-Schools"), as we all know, is the intellectual phase of a woman's life, that time when, unencumbered by societal expectations or hormonal rages, one may pursue any curiosity from the mysteries of a yo-yo to the meaning of infinity. These two particular pursuits were where I left off in the fifth grade when I discovered a hair growing in the wrong place and all hell broke loose.

Galhood is that time when a woman's life is hopelessly complicated by the acquisition of feminine wiles. Some are culturally induced, some are biologically induced, and some are the work of Young and Rubicam. My junkpile of a mind is chock full of Lady Clairol and Toni dolls and dungaree dolls and women who dreamt they were Something in their Maidenform bras. These details form the backdrop of memories in such pieces as "2Good 2Be 4Gotten."

I came to consciousness in the 1950s, when galhood was in flower. I saw galhood undergo a crisis as we turned into 100 percent natural hippie mommas. I saw galhood trashed and denounced by feminism, a confusing time for guys and gals alike. And finally, I saw galhood's greatest achievement (or darkest dream): today's New Ultra Yuppie Woman. I trace the evolution of *Homo yupicus* in "Where Have All the Yuppies Gone?"

I'm not sure when I began to pass into old girlhood. I know it is a time when one can return to the intellectual life tempered by a mixture of nostalgia for the concerns of galhood and gratitude that one is no longer fettered by them. Still, I think Joan Collins and Linda Evans are enjoying this more than I am.

Sometime after my mother died or my two daughters were born, I began to feel myself sliding back into the freedom of imagination I had known before that fateful day in 1957 when Vince Tumbarelli put his arm around me. I guess I began to realize my feminine wiles—which I never intentionally used, swear to God—were fading. The actual rite of passage occurred last week, when I was walking down the street and all the young men approaching me were saying the same thing. Instead of "Hey baby, want to boogie?" they asked, "Spare change?"

Anticipating how this change from gal to old fart might affect me, I returned to my girlhood dream—I became a writer when I grew up. I never understood why I listed my ambition in kindergarten as "writer," because I couldn't even sign my name at the time. But as the fortieth birthday loomed larger I began to pour my little heart out and let it bleed on paper. Of course, I had always written but I never took it seriously. It was a way of life, not a living.

I didn't really see where the kind of sadder but wiseass stuff I liked to write fit into the landscape of writing for profit. I filled my life with jobs—teacher, nurse, mother—good woman's work. Being a nurse (my career until a few months ago) gave me access to the human heart and gastrointestinal tract in a manner that few writers, let alone human beings, get to know. This nurses' way of knowledge, the view from the gal in knee-length white polyester, is presented in the piece "The End Is Near."

I never got serious about publishing until I discovered the alternative press. It used to be the underground press and some now call it the "life-style" press, but it represented, for me, a place where I could lay my hat and take off my gloves.

In my community, Berkeley, California (a town that has been much mythologized as America's experiment in socialist surrealism), the paper is *The East Bay Express.* Like papers in every town where there's an art cinema and an espresso machine, it is distributed free each week and contains an entertainment guide, ads for futons, exercise classes, computers, and psychotherapy, and the kind of writing you seldom find in magazines or daily newspapers. Thus it was that my life became an open free newspaper.

There probably are few communities outside of Berkeley that would nurture a writer the way I have been nurtured here. (The byplay between writer and reader is described in "Turning Forty.") Berkeley is a community that values the California ethic of earnest confessional approaches to intimacy ("Hi, my name is Rick. I favor divestment and have a problem with premature ejaculation. Who are you?"). But it is also a place that feels as alienated from the American mainstream as the average artist with half a brain. It is a place where readers of a paper like the *Express* could tolerate a satirical fantasy like "All in a Day's Work," an imagined day in the life of a Hollywood coroner. However, even I was shocked when I saw that the editor chose to highlight the following quote in the middle of the page: "I thought I told you never to bring up Monroe's vagina at the dinner table."

Coming from this background, my transition to the mainstream press has been difficult. In my attempt to come up from the minors, my first piece for the *San Francisco Chronicle* was "Legacy of the Oval Bed," in which I suggested that the main accomplishment of the Reagan administration is that he satisfies his [old] lady. Unfortunately, some vocal readers reacted as if I had done a scandalous investigative piece on the president's sex life.

The process of becoming a public person, a newspaper columnist, has been a strange one. Thoughts that I kept to myself for decades are now debated by people for literary merit, moral worth, and political correctness. People who only wanted an enema from Alice Kahn the nurse now ask to meet Alice Kahn the writer.

Recently at a party, I was introduced to a woman who said she was dying to meet me. As she shook my hand and told me how much she admired my work, I looked at her in horror and said, "Mary, you've known me for ten years. Our daughters went to nursery school together. We stood side by side and passed out trail mix. I jogged by your house and waved every day for seven years!"

Local politicians who never gave a damn about me now want my endorsement on their campaign statements: Alice Kahn, cynical, asocial critic urges that you support Joe Schmo for Rent Board.

And, finally, there are the love letters. Those have been really astounding. One man wrote telling me all the deep hidden stuff he saw in me and he even included his impressive curriculum vitae. I wrote back and said he had no idea what a turn-on an M.A. from Georgetown was but where the hell was he on that rainy night in 1964 when I really needed him?

No doubt about it, I brought this on myself. Oh, sure, I told myself all along that all I cared about was engaging the uninterested reader. But I have never been able to shake a certain little girl who couldn't get what she wanted. What I wanted as a child was simple enough—constant attention. But Silky, my father, was busy with his regrets and Fonzo, my mother, was busy with her beet borscht.

As a young woman, I wanted men from Elvis Presley to Professor Windenbag (the lyric poetry maven) to want me, need me, love me. Now, in my young old age, I beg the reader: Take a look, gimme a chance, watch me now. I can do satire, I can do sentiment, I can do social criticism. I can do the jerk! Why else am I slaving over a hot disk drive except for your affection?

I

Crazy Little Thing
Called Love

2Good 2Be 4Gotten

One summer night, do you remember one summer night? It was prom night, June 16, 1961. You-ou and I-yi-yi, in the backseat of Larry's Merc.

Following a massive search, my best friend Penny had helped me find *the* dress. It had three tiers of organza over white silk shantung. The top was embossed with velveteen flowers and there was a skinny velvet sash at my skinny little waist. All that grapefruit and Diet-Rite pop paid off. Because it was strapless, I got a white lace strapless bra to go with it. You know, like Madonna made famous—only without the dress.

It was a time not unlike the present—obsessed with hair and underwear. I got my hair done that afternoon at Fabulous Vic's. My limp locks were teased into a bouffant flip with pixie bangs. Jackie Kennedy meets Audrey Hepburn. "You look *fab*-u-lous," said Vic himself.

"They'll eat you up with a spoon."

I came home and put on the album from *West Side Story*. Singing "I Feel Pretty," I shaved my legs from the ankle to the panty line. I lay back on the bed and stretched out my legs like Chita Rivera and slid on my nylons. Then, standing there in my crinoline, bra, and three-inch spike heels, I put peroxide and soap flakes on my arms to bleach the hair. I plucked my eyebrows and sprayed my armpits—"One squeeze puts your mind at ease"—and doused my neck with Evening in Paris. They're gonna eat me up with a spoon.

We were saying farewell to old Senn High in Chicago, our class of five hundred. I hoped I'd win the contest for naming the prom. The only thing I'd ever won in my life was a free ticket to the junior prom for naming it "Kismet." But Wheezer won it for "Some Enchanted Evening." I did, however, write the poem for the prom booklet—four stanzas—the first beginning with "Some," the second with "Enchanted," and the third with "Evening." Then the last stanza:

> *Some Enchanted Evening*
> *We'll meet again.*
> *To laugh.*
> *To cry.*
> *To think about Senn.*
> *Some Enchanted Evening*
> *by Kismet's call*
> *We'll stand together*
> *At the End of it All.*

I hated Wheezer and I'll tell you why. She was class treasurer and I was secretary. (Usually, I ran for sergeant-at-arms, the joke being that as the biggest loudmouth in the class, I could tell myself to shut up.) But Wheezer shut my mouth one day when she came up to me and asked me if I liked this boy who was vice-president of the class. How could she tell? Just because I never missed student council? Just because I hung around his locker? Just because I wrote his name with fancy curlicues in my notebook?

"Yeah, I like him," I blurted.

"Well," she said after I fessed up, "I'm going to ask him to the senior prom."

What could I say? I was heartbroken. Wheezer was a winner. She once showed me her big fat scrapbook full of blue ribbons, blue ribbons in everything—sports, academics, citizenship. She was even in the court for prom queen. Besides that, I couldn't compete with her. I cut my cultural teeth on *True Confessions* stories in which two girls fight over a boy and one ends up pouring acid on the other.

All was lost. I was on the verge of that adolescent flirtation with death. I ran home and consoled myself with Dion's "A Teenager in Love" and Ricky Nelson's "A Teenager's Romance," and Del Shannon singing "Runaway."

But the boy asked me! I was stunned. One day, I hid near his locker to see if it was just accident—kismet—that we met. No, he was waiting for me. He's so shy, I thought. Then he uttered the unforgettable words "Wanna go?" and the words were like music.

I tried not to gloat around Wheezer. She ended up going with Hal Bressler, who all the boys called "Betty Ballser." Wheezer and Ballser, Wheezer and Ballser; ha-ha-ha-ha-ha.

The first one hundred couples to buy tickets always got their names in the school paper. For this, Karl Sonkin and I, who were features editors, wrote our magnum opus—a two hundred–line poem of rhymed couplets incorporating all the names:

> *Look out guys, there's no way to please her*
> *Here comes Hal with his girl Wheezer*

On prom night, the boy came for me with a wrist corsage in his hand. His father bought it wholesale that afternoon and the orchid was already dead. "That's okay," I said, and put it on next to my mustard seed bracelet, over my little white gloves.

We doubled with Larry and Merle, Lutch and Merky. Lutch was driving his brand-new white Mercury Comet, the first of a new style of compact cars. We had the backseat. *The backseat.* Oh, baby, baby.

A week later, when I was in the front seat next to Lutch, we got in a big accident. We were in the middle of a ten-car pile-up on the Outer Drive and the Merc was totaled. At the moment of impact, as the compact collapsed like an accordion between a Caddie and a Buick, my face slammed into the windshield, which spiderwebbed before me. We came out unscathed.

All my friends went down to the junkyard to look at the Merc and see my lipstick print—Revlon's Hot Coral—on the shattered glass. Everyone said I had survived "the kiss of death."

That summer I started to think of myself as lucky. Always before, I carried this two-ton chip on my shoulder labeled "lousy childhood" and felt handicapped against the Wheezers of the world. But now, I was going to college, I had the boy, and I had survived the kiss of death. And on prom night, the backseat of the Merc was just so fine.

We didn't drink. We never saw marijuana. We were almost all virgins except for an occasional boy who was rumored to have come of age at a Gypsy storefront or a girl so rich she could dare to be "fast." Before the prom, we had a "Coke-tail" party at Lutch's. It was only for the guys in Hearts Club and their dates. Hearts Club—Dave, Art, Gary, Don, Eddie, and Larry—were just the boys who played hearts every night if their girlfriends would let them. We girls bought them skinny black ties mono-grammed with their initials enclosed in a little heart. It was my idea. The boy never wore his. Too sissy.

The prom itself was held in the M and M room—the Merchants and Manufacturers Room—of the enormous Merchandise Mart. We only spent about two hours of the fifteen-hour date at the prom proper. There was a terribly square band. The only hit song they could play was "Moon River," which was number one at the time. Hardly anybody danced. Mostly you promenaded about looking cool. The boy bought me a Coke and we sat in a corner talking about George Bernard Shaw and Nietzsche and Hegel. We were about to be collegiate.

After the appearance at the prom, we left for our elegant meal at the Pump Room. Lutch ordered steak tartare. "That sounds elegant," we all agreed. I think stunned silence is the way to describe his face when the pile of raw hamburger was set before him. To make up for it, he ordered cherries jubilee. We all panicked when we saw the flames.

We stopped to pick up some burgers and shakes—the elegant food was all yuck—then went back home, changed into our Bermudas, and met back at the lake. There was an awful smell. Hundreds of dead fish had washed up on the sand. We didn't know the words *ecological disaster* yet, so we set up our blankets and volleyball nets and pretended nothing was happening. The boy and I left Stinkfish Beach and went back into the trees and made out all night. Under a moon of love.

When the sun came up, the gang went out for breakfast. We sat around the big orange Naugahyde booth eating deep-dish apple pie and signing our yearbooks. Karl wrote: "Alice, I am so happy that you were able to go to the prom and, of course, share so many happy moments with that fabulous guy, for, to see you happy—even tho my own heart at times was breaking—is a fulfillment of my basic aim this last semester. . . ." Wheezer wrote: "I think that you know the feeling I have for you so I don't have to say too much except that I will never forget you." Merky wrote: "I pray the Lord will watch over you and keep you well. Your friend till I have no breath left in my body. . . ." And a boy named Burt, whom I talked to once, wrote: "I remember a day not long ago when the whole world looked black to me. But with you, on that day, when we discussed myself I felt a ray of light permeate myself. I shall never forget you as long as I live because for you I have truly felt this feeling called 'spiritual love.' "

The boy wouldn't sign. He said it was "too personal."

With few exceptions, I never saw any of them again. As class secretary, I was supposed to organize a reunion. I held on to the five hundred postcards I took home on graduation day until the four-cent stamps became antique and the addresses obsolete.

We scattered all over the country. Lutch lives in New York. Merky, I heard, struck it rich and now lives in Boca Raton. Penny's a born-again Christian in a suburb of Dallas. Wheezer, I read, is a computer consultant in New Haven. Burt teaches philosophy at a small New England college. Karl I see on TV sometimes, reporting the news on Channel 4. And me and the boy are still going together, raising little girls in Berkeley.

People assume it's been happily-ever-aftersville between here and high school, as if the broken china platter and the torn Boston fern and the "I'm going out and maybe I'll be back" had never occurred. People want to know the secret. Was it luck? Was it kismet? Was it a mutual hallucination? It's a question as old as Frankie Lymon: Why do fools fall in love? All I can say is that the night was young and the moon was mellow and the leaves came tumbling down.

Desperately Seeking
. . . Anyone

YOUNG WHITE URBAN MALE into radical politics but not from an ideological standpoint or an obnoxious activist approach, likes hiking in the woods on a rainy day but hates California (it's cold and damp) although unwilling to relocate. Not into spirituality or growth but believes there is a supreme intelligence that could be guiding the universe although isn't. Likes reading nineteenth-century French poets (in translation) and Anything by Larry McMurtry. Hates never having to say "I'm sorry." Into Amadeus, Miles, and Springsteen. An eclectic kinda guy. Can cook stir-fry or Weber dome barbecue only. Does own laundry but only with Ivory due to long-standing jock-itch situation. Seeks young woman (15 to 25) for afternoon of violin concerto in E, Fumé Blanc, and quiet talk about reducing nuclear risk.

YOUNG (DEPENDING ON YOUR definition) midsize city semiprofessional woman seeks one good man. Into aerobic meditation, the New Catholicism, veggie cuisine, and all-around whole-grain approach to life. I like dry, hot climates—the desert or the beach when the sun is blazing. Hate—absolutely despise—Larry McMurtry, Miles Davis, California wine, French poetry, jocks, political guilt trips. I don't want to meet with you, eat or sleep or bo-peep with you, proselytize you, cannibalize you, bring you down, or call in the clowns. All I really want to do, is baby be friends with you.

YOUNG BUT MATURING, LEARNING, reaching-out-and-touching-some-one man interested in change. Wants a friend. A friend is all I've ever wanted. Really. Swear to supreme intelligence that ought to be guiding universe that friendship is the main thing I seek in a young, New Catholic woman. *Likes* woman who can stand her own ground. *Wants* a challenge. Wants a woman who knows what she likes and isn't afraid to say it. But no ballbusting feminist stereotypical left-wing nightmare women please.

OVER 30 (LET'S GET honest) attractive woman who likes to clean her house while exercising stone naked to Kenny Loggins music questions use of term *ballbuster*. Suggests undue amount of para-noia bordering on misogyny. Goes along with whole macho im-age conjured by mentioning Baudelaire and Bruce Springsteen. Into boots of Spanish leather. But warn you: Potential for these boots to do a Nancy Sinatra all over you.

RECEDING HAIRLINE BUT WHO'S to worry? Into *boots!* Are you kid-ding, I love boots. Boots is my life. Never mentioned Baudelaire by name. In fact, more of a Rimbaud kinda guy. Come to think of it, I like Cardinal Newman, Cesar Chavez, peace in El Salvador, and quiet walks in the woods in the rain but will consider the desert. Willing to relocate to the desert. Willing to try quiet walks in the rain in the desert. Driven wild by image of nude woman doing aerobic dusting. Come back, baby, I want to clean house with you.

EXERCISE TO HOLD LID on middle-age spread. Breasts starting to sag regardless of Joannie Greggins armlifts × 10. Hate the rain. Get severely depressed, worse than premenstrual, if it rains on my birthday. Please don't quote Elvis Presley lyrics. Reminds me of grammar school. Never picked for teams. Refused to give up candy for Lent. Got pimples. Unpopular. Created own bad rep in high school but for naught. Nobody tried to cop nothing. Still interested?

LONELY KINDA GUY DOESN'T care about grammar school or high school grief. Doesn't even care about high-priced spread (not too bad, is it?). Get out your boots. In the words of the immortal Pat Boone: April love can drip right off your fingers.

WIMPY WOMAN WONDERS WHAT all that talk about wanting strong woman was all about. What about boots bit? Would it matter to lonely kinda guy if wimpy kinda woman had actually lied about boots bit and, in fact, cleans house in dirty pink bunny slippers and chenille bathrobe?

AGING MAN WANTS to get laid.

YOUR SPACE OR MINE?

Porno-to-Go

I'll do anything to be one of the masses. Why else did I watch Fergie get married or read *Elvis and Me* or see every goddamn misery series that comes on TV? Do you think I like these things? No, but I'm a people person. That's why I read *People*. That's why I dream of seeing Frank in Vegas. That's why—and that's the only reason why—I rented a porno video.

I just can't stand to miss out on a mass experience. So when I read that watching porn on the VCR had become as middle-class American as wanting to whip Muammar Qaddafi's ass, I said: Who am I to question the will of the people? And, what with the government Commission on Pornography threatening to find scientific evidence linking pornography and violence, I figured I'd better see what this is all about before you need a white coat and a degree in physics to get your hands on one of those dirty cassettes.

There were two things that had stopped me from renting a porno flick in the past. The first was fear that I'd get one of those horrible super sicko violent movies and I'd hate myself for contributing—even in the interest of being just folks—to such an industry. I'd heard the sad stories of decent people who just wanted a little nooky-plus movie ending up with heavy metal meets Charlie Manson.

See, you can't judge a porno movie by its cover. Sure some things are obvious. A title like *Big Boy's Buns on Bikes* is somewhat genre-suggestive. But other titles like *Behind the Green Door* are pretty ambiguous. *Behinds Behind the Green Door*—that's a little clearer.

The second thing that stopped me was the fear that I'd be seen. As if my reputation with the right-ons wasn't in enough jeopardy, all I needed was to be caught with *Deep Throat* in my hands. "Don't you know that woman was forced and tortured into making that movie?" "Of course I do. I'm not watching it for pleasure. I'm watching it to prove I'm not a snob. The masses love it."

As I slipped incognito into the video parlor, the first person I saw was a prominent local intellectual. Before I got embarrassed at being almost caught, I began to wonder if perhaps he himself was not there for a similar nefarious purpose. Maybe instead of *My Dinner With Andre* he was going after *My Petit Dejeuner With Andrea?* Why assume an intellectual was above the scumline of ordinary people? As I headed into that little Adults Only alcove I began to wonder who I'd find there. Probably librarians, professors, bookstore owners—culture peddlers by day, smut seekers by night.

But no, I was alone. The only Adult in Berkeley.

Almost randomly and for no explicable reason, I chose *Beverly Hills Exposed.* There weren't any whips on the cassette cover and it seemed to be geared toward a nonspecialty audience. That was enough. I mean, what can you expect, the *Good Housekeeping* seal of approval?

Entering my home, I carefully placed it in its plain plastic cover in a remote corner of my room for viewing after the children were asleep. But like a bee to honey, within five minutes my precocious preteen was asking, "What's *Beverly Hills Exposed?*"

"Oh, just some dumb movie," I said.

"Not an adult movie, Mom," she said in that you've-let-me-down tone. Caught. I restrained myself from making a remark about how at least it wasn't one of those Molly Ringwald guess-who's-got-her-period movies.

Good golly, Miss Molly, next to the acting in *Beverly Hills Exposed*, you're a regular Ingrid Bergman. But let's be perfectly clear. Acting is not what this kind of movie is about. Plot is not what this kind of movie is about. And certainly cinematography is not where it's at either, although there are some close-up shots that will knock your socks off.

Nevertheless, despite the lack of any of the usual cinematic graces, I would say this movie afforded me at least as much—and quite probably more—pleasure than any Woody Allen movie I've ever seen. Much as I love the Woodman, I have never felt literally compelled to use the pause button during one of his movies. Now I understand why decent people wouldn't go see these films in porno movie houses. Who can have sex in a room full of men in dirty trenchcoats?

This is definitely a watch-at-home-with-your-favorite-guy-or-doll (or both) situation. You don't need a William ("Mr. New Criticism") Empson to know which way the wind blows in this movie. There is not one type of ambiguity. You watch it as a stimulant or you have your head examined.

Let's face it, for old married couples things are not what they once were. After two or three or eighteen years of marriage, the sparks that once flew at the mere touch of a hand can no longer take you to Masters and Johnson's Stage Three.

To review, Masters and Johnson discovered that a sexual act consists of five stages.

1. Thinking about it.
2. Getting hot.
3. Almost home.
4. Climax.
5. What's in the fridge?

A porno flick serves no other artistic purpose than to fast-forward the first three stages. The real question, then, is how much of a degenerate do you end up feeling like for having fallen for it.

I personally am not an advocate of "whatever turns you on." Whatever turns you on, in my opinion, has opened the door for rape, night stalkers, the lingerie explosion, Nancy Reagan, and a lot of other modern dilemmas. *Beverly Hills Exposed*, thank goodness, featured no particular violence. It was just a day in the life of a normal Bev Hills couple who sleep with everything they can get their privates on. He does it to the maid and the secretary. She does it to the exercise coach. Anyone who remembers the old joke that finishes with the punch line "We're the Aristocrats" knows the plot to this movie.

My only criticism of the movie—aside from no script, no direction, no acting (my husband used the term *fucked out* to characterize the cast)—was a minor one. Without going into a detailed structural analysis, I must point out that the parallel three-way scenes did seem truly sexist. In the two-girls-and-a-guy one, the girls mix it up; but in the two-guys-and-a-girl one, the guys make a painstaking effort never, ever to touch each other. Loosen up, guys. At least wink at each other while you're straddling the same fence. I also question the bizarre porno movie convention of documenting male orgasm with close-ups of old faithful erupting.

Why, then, if it was "good for you," the reader may ask, am I not rushing out to rent another one? I think the simple answer is fear of dependency. There is a real danger of conditioning with sex. Making love can begin to resemble the old game of "I'm going on a trip and I'm going to take . . ." when the list of prerequisites gets too long. If you must have a movie *and* a garter belt *and* a vibrator *and Bolero and* a few lines of cocaine *and* a whip *and* handcuffs, etc., etc., every time you have sex, then, as the late great Ricky Nelson almost said, "I'd rather park a truck."

Tragedy of the Single Man

With grim determination, Norm Noodleman, forty, single, contemplates his future. Results of a disturbing new study from Bob Jones University indicate that single men over thirty-five have a 3 percent chance of being turned into sausage.

For those over forty, the results are even grimmer. Once he hits two score, a man's chance of being turned into sausage goes up to 6 percent. What could be wurst? Get this: By the time a single man is one hundred, he stands a whopping 22 percent chance of ending up as dead meat.

The implications are not lost on Noodleman, an unemployed performance artist who ekes out a living as part owner of a thriving launderette.

"If you're a single man," he said, "there's no escaping this study. My mother back in Jersey sent it to me. My father called me from his convalescent home in Miami and asked if I'd heard. You can hardly pick up a paper without reading about our plight.

"It's all we talk about in my men's group. I'm getting to the point where I can't even phone up a woman. Why bother?"

Noodleman is not alone. In bars, at baseball games, in bathrooms and other places where single men gather, the Bob Jones study is the number one topic of conversation.

At Candlestick Park, Jeff Lorimer, thirty-six, single, stares strangely at his kielbasa. Lorimer says he tries to be philosophical about it. "I have to go on with my life. If they're gonna grind you down, they're gonna grind you down."

At the Washington Square Bar and Grill, Dr. Sydney H. Saigan, forty-two, single, takes a different approach to the news. Saigan, dean of the Life Sciences Department at the University of California, says that as a result of the study he is finally living his life to its fullest.

"The main thing the Jones boys did was get me off my duff and into stuff. I've just met this beautiful woman, and we're going to her place or mine," Saigan said, referring to an attractive blonde clinging to his jacket. He says he is planning a book about his experiences called *Enjoy Yourself and Still Come Out a Wiener*.

The problem quantified in the Bob Jones study is particularly pronounced for men living in the San Francisco area, where the large number of sausage factories and outlets poses additional concern.

Gay Jones (no relation to Bob), owner of Gourmet Charcuterie on Noe Street, says that because he is married he is not concerned. But he says a number of single male employees have quit their jobs because of anxieties raised by the study. "They feel that being here in Sausage Central puts them particularly at risk."

A recent cover story in *Newsweak* created a wave of panic among single men across the nation. A major issue raised by the story is whether single men should have children given their pathetic, hopeless situation. "If you took all the single men who are worried about this and lined them up, end to end, you'd have enough hot dogs to feed football fans for the next five seasons."

One positive note comes from Mona Wimmins, a therapist who specializes in the tragedy of single men. "Men can't let newspaper stories and university studies run their lives," said Wimmins.

Lest single men rush out and get engaged, hoping to beat the odds, a recent study done at the California Academy of Culinary Arts suggests the folly of a knee-jerk wedding. According to Wimmins, "The academy found that men who marry have a hundred percent greater chance of being pounded into pâté."

Modern Romance
The Eight Commandments of Love

It's not exactly the chapel of Love, but a Unitarian Church will certainly do as the place to learn the gospel according to Rich Gosse, a self-described "nationally recognized expert on the singles life-style." The Lord has not placed Gosse on this earth to make people better or to teach them a lesson or to raise hell or consciousness. The Lord has called Rich Gosse to help us *spiel* our way into "a loving relationship."

I found Gosse in the church meeting room seated on one of the green, brown, and orange polyester couches. He is not unattractive: tall and slim with brown curly hair and a puckish smile. He wore a form-fitting shirt with the top two buttons open so we got a hint of chest hair and a figure free from unwanted cellulite. His skin, pitted and scarred from acne, suggested a painful adolescence.

I had come to the seminar looking not for love but for a fun story—the carefree world of the legion of swinging bachelors and bachelorettes—and, in particular, for Rich Gosse's eight foolproof rules for finding love. Instead, I found myself in a lonely place—a room clouded with unfulfillment and self-doubt. It wasn't sexy; it was poignant. I had stumbled into one of those Nathanael West and Edward Hopper places in the heart.

Seated opposite Gosse on the dumpy couch were the devotees, two women who had paid ten dollars for the four-hour seminar. There was Nancy, an attractive woman with the kind of blue eyes and blond curly hair I spent my childhood envying, and Marie, an equally attractive Frenchwoman who, I found out later, had her own successful import business. Both women appeared to be over forty and neither had ever been married. When they discussed the serious business of looking for love, they did not smile very much. Several other women showed up, looked around at the slim pickings malewise, acted surprised by the ten-dollar admission fee, and left. About a half hour into the seminar, in between Rule Number One and Rule Number Two, a man entered.

He was as close to the generic man as I'd ever seen—short brown hair, brown eyes, pale white skin, brown shoes, gray socks, blue slacks, white shirt, green jacket with folded white handkerchief. He seldom spoke and then only with hesitation. Often, his sentences didn't make sense. He bit his fingernails throughout the seminar and was, I believe, clinically depressed. When Nancy and Marie described their varied experiences with personals ads, the man, Steven, said he had had only one response: "Many women called but for some reason they all hung up."

Supplying a leitmotiv at the seminar was Dorothy, a chubby sixty-year-old widow from Montana, who is Rich Gosse's secretary and sidekick. Dorothy comes to the seminars because, she said, "I enjoy it." With gray hair, black-framed spectacles, a paisley skirt, white blouse, tiny pearl earrings, and wedgie shoes, Dorothy is the very essence of a gal—as normal a person as has been seen in our town in years. When, about twenty minutes into the seminar, Rich Gosse explained that unattractive people can't expect to bag attractive mates, Dorothy turned to me and said, "What are you looking for, sweetie?"

Just the facts, ma'am, I explained, and the rules. I'm a writer. I don't look for love. I look for stories and the story here was that a man was about to reveal eight infallible rules for finding love and only three people had come to listen.

You might think that Rich Gosse would be discouraged by the poor turnout and the fact that he paid forty dollars rent, promised a four-hour seminar, and received only thirty dollars cash money. But no. He is, by trade, a computer salesman, steeled to rejection, and resiliently he plunged into his talk, making no effort to "know" the audience, to have them say who they were and why they were there. A "motor mouth" since Catholic school, Gosse had no problem lecturing to three hopeful women and a hopeless male. Besides, as he acknowledged later, Nancy and Marie were "better than average looking."

Before he got to the Eight Commandments, the how-tos of meeting people, Gosse ran through the specific places where singles gather. "The biggest singles group in the area," Gosse began, "is Shipmates, which often draws five hundred people out to the First Presbyterian Church." Throughout the lecture Gosse extolled the virtues of church groups and churches as places to look for love. "Churches are especially good for men because they're loaded with women. . . . The Unitarian Church is beautiful because they all have singles groups and they don't believe in anything. . . . You don't have to be a member of a group to go to their singles groups, but if you can't stand Lutherans, stay out of Lutheran churches; if you can't stand Jews, stay out of Jewish community centers.

"People are always convinced their community is the worst for singles," Gosse said. "But the San Francisco area is the best. It has the highest per capita number of singles, much better than Omaha. We dominate the Bay Area—it ought to be easy. But singles are crybabies, always complaining. The worst are women in San Francisco who claim all the men are married, gay, or jerks."

Rule 1

It is this critical attitude that explains why loneliness is the coat we wear. We have violated Rule Numero Uno: Have Realistic Expectations. The problem, said Gosse, is essentially that nobody wants a jerk, and everybody wants Tom Selleck or a *Playboy* bunny. "Only five percent of us are born beautiful, wealthy and with a good personality. Ninety-five percent of us are chasing after this five percent. Men expect, number one, good looks in women. Ditto number two. Ditto number three. For women, number one is money—which may not apply to the city of Berkeley, which is the most liberated in the United States—but the aphrodisiacs for most women are money, status, and power."

"But that's superficial," complained Marie in her charming French accent.

"Today, we're talking generalizations," responded Gosse. Although one suspects that for him there's no tomorrow.

Lower your expectations, insists the Jerry Brown of love. "Make a list of everything you're looking for, your ideal mate, and hold it up and say: 'I'm never going to get involved with someone like this.'" Following the power of negative thinking, we got a little creeping Marin Countyism: "I had this problem," Gosse confessed. "I would be attracted to a woman who didn't meet my expectations and therefore I would not get involved. I had to learn to *give myself permission* to be attracted to people who I am attracted to."

Others, he cautioned, may be fatally attracted to the wrong type. Some women, for example, repeatedly get involved with alcoholic men. They may need "the Alan Alda type, as they're known in the business." Come to think of it, Gosse may be an Alan Alda type himself. He proudly explained that he never refuses a dance with women who attend his singles events. He is what is known in the business as a mercy dancer.

RULE 2

This rule is directed at single women, who Gosse claims stay home every night: Get Out of the House. "People always ask me, 'Rich, how often do I have to go out of the house looking for love?' As often as possible, I tell them. People are lazy about looking for love. It's hard work. How many hours are you willing to spend looking for love?"

RULE 3

More important than getting out of the house is learning to violate the basic law of childhood: Don't talk to strangers. This is Rule Number Three: Hang Around Strangers as Much as Possible. When I raised the rape risk issue—and I didn't even mention the sex-disease screening problem—Rich seemed surprised and explained that men can be raped too. "Oh, yes," piped up our gal Dorothy. "I read about a case in England. A woman chained a man to a bed. It was wonderful."

"I don't know how we got off on this," said Rich, returning to his discourse on the pros and cons of singles bars.

"Singles bars do have lots of people looking for love. I interviewed lots of make-out artists, you know—the guys with the gold chains . . ." our unchained expert explained, "and every single one of them was looking for love. Of course, that's not to say they didn't want to get laid that night."

RULE 4

Better places for serious looking were revealed in a discussion of Rule Number Four: Hang Around People of the Opposite Sex. Looking for love is hard work, we were again cautioned: "It isn't fun." What terrible news! Even in lace valentine land, it's still no pain, no gain. "If you want love, you have to pay the price, and

women's lib—outside of Berkeley and New York—is a myth."
Men like to hang around men doing masculine things and women
like to do things men hate to do.

Why, I wondered, was Gosse addressing these remarks my
way? I asked him how he knew he was in a feminist stronghold.
"They wear less feminine clothes," he said. "In Marin County,
the women are no different than Peoria."

I had done my best to disguise my feminism beneath a pink and
beige facade. I had left my Birkenstocks at home. But Gosse is a
single-minded animal. He sensed my lack of desperation. Later, I
asked him how feminist strongholds stack up next to other places
for singles. "They're good places" for leftist-lib-type guys. The
main advantage is that women pick up the check.

"The number one place to meet women," he continued, looking at the pallid Steven, who never makes eye contact, "is to take
an aerobics class. The ratio is ten to one, but it does hurt a lot.
Folk dancing is good. Women love it. There's a three-to-one ratio
there. A sewing class is good too. Remember, you're not there to
learn to sew. You're looking for love."

Women, Gosse said, should hang around softball games or basketball courts. "You don't have to play. You're looking for love."
And go back to school. "Call Adult Ed and ask, 'Which class has
the most men?' Remember, your purpose is not to learn anything.
Your purpose is to meet men."

Gosse rolled off more numbers, like a man selling computers.
Although friends are the number one way people meet, jobs are
number two. "Ten percent of all people meet their husbands or
wives on the job. Public service is good, like a bank teller. My
cousin met her husband at a bank. Of course, it ended in divorce." Dorothy checked in with another advantage to meeting
people while a bank teller. "Then you'll know how much money
they have," she said, chuckling and reaching in her handbag for a
Rolo.

The third place people find their mates are singles bars and
singles groups. Gosse went through the leading singles groups

from Sierra Singles to Smokeless Singles to Divorce Recovery Workshops. He also discussed the unorthodox methods (in the supermarket: "Crash your cart into them. They'll notice you"). He ran through the pluses and minuses of Parents Without Partners ("Problem is you have to have a child") and photo, video, and computer dating ("People lie to computers so you have the garbage-in, garbage-out problem"). But his personal favorite singles groups are political organizations. "The number one reason people volunteer is to meet people. On election night, I go to every victory party. If I go to one and it's no fun, I go to the opposite candidate's. The Republicans are good because they're rich and usually have good bands. If I don't meet someone there I go to the Democrats. But then, I'm very politically involved."

RULE 5

All this hustling will, alas, come to naught without following Rule Number Five: Initiate Contact. Here Gosse showed his toughness in the jungle of love. "The more times you get rejected, the more scar tissue you build up. You build up scar tissue by going out there and getting bloody." Women, he insisted, must overcome their reluctance. "Men love forward women. You're not rejected because men don't like forward women—they just don't like you." Of course, he allowed, if you just wait till 2:00 A.M., when the bars are closing down, a man will contact you, "but we all know what that's like. . . ."

Here I found the discussion getting oppressively sad. I couldn't look at Nancy and Marie. During the break I said to Marie, "You're so terrific. Why are you here?" She's tan, she's smart, she's slim, she's articulate, she's got her own business—for chrissakes, she's French! "I don't know," she said with pain, "I don't know." I felt clumsy for having blurted out the sixty-four-dollar question.

Gosse continued with the major problem people have in initiating contact. They can't think of an opening line. Any line will do, he insisted. " 'Hi, I'm a jerk.' That will do. If you say it to enough people, some will respond." That, of course, is easy for Rich Gosse to say. He is, in a sense, the unordained spokesperson for Jerks' Lib.

"No," insisted Marie, she could never say, "Hi, I'm a jerk." "How about: 'Hi, I'm a French jerk?' " I offered.

At this point, Steven took out a dog-eared index card from his coat pocket and wrote something down. I wondered whether that night he would go home, look in the mirror and say repeatedly, "Hi, I'm a jerk."

RULE 6

Finally, having initiated contact, we get to Rule Number Six: Get Involved in as Many Superficial Conversations as Possible. "I talk to people all the time and they say to me, 'Rich, I'm not afraid to initiate contact, but we get involved in these superficial, bullshit conversations, not meaningful, personal, exciting stuff. . . .' [They forget] superficial conversation is good. It allows people to graduate to the next level of intimate conversation. You can't talk about hating singles bars or the pain of being dumped until you develop common ground like weather, Ronald Reagan —superficial things."

RULE 7

Rule Seven, Get Personal, admitted Gosse, goes against the grain. Most people are taught it's rude and must learn the secret of getting personal. "You want to pry and you want to reveal. The secret is to do both at the same time. Pry and reveal. Pry and reveal." For instance, you run into someone who you've heard just broke up with her boyfriend but you're not sure. Here's how you do it in the world according to Gosse. You say, "I was living with someone last year and I got dumped and it was painful for me, so I want to know 'did your association with so and so end sadly too?' "

"You see," said Gosse, "you can't just ask: 'Did you get dumped?' "

Rule 8

At last we came to Rule Eight, and although I was getting weary, Gosse had not run out of gas. He got up a head of steam and roared into the narrative. "Okay, now for the biggie. *Intimacy* begins. After all those boring conversations and all those losers you've met someone. The fun begins. You're both attracted. You're enjoying each other. It's all working and you're thinking: 'I sure am glad I went to the Looking for Love seminar.' But now the bar is closing, it's turned cold at the beach, the baseball game is over. It's the moment of truth and you must make a decision whether or not to see each other again. It's a game of chicken and the loser says, 'It's been fun. Hope I see you again.' And *that* is the tragedy that gets acted over and over again."

There was a moment of silence and everyone breathed heavily with the weight of remembrance. Gosse, the consummate salesman, went in for the kill. "Rule Eight: Pin Them Down for Your Next Contact! All is lost without this." Trading phone numbers, he insisted, is also "a tragedy" because "ninety percent lose the nerve or the number to call. I hear women say all the time, 'I rush home from work and the asshole never calls.' You've got to pin them down."

The group sat uncomfortably still. The Moses of possible matrimony had revealed all eight commandments. Nancy sighed. Marie bobbed her head up and down as if she knew what had to be done. Steven chewed on his cuticles. I furiously took notes. Dorothy grinned at us and Rich asked, "Any questions?"

"Yes," said Nancy. "What is the ratio of heterosexual men to women?"

Rich reveled in the numbers. At birth, there are more boys

than girls. "By age thirty-five," he said, "it equals out, and then after thirty-five the men start dropping off like flies, so that by sixty it's three and a half single women to every man." The message for Steven is clear: If he can just hold on, he'll be hot.

On the other hand, Gosse, who is thirty-six, offered advice to women over forty; advice that, he acknowledged, gets him into trouble with feminists: "One: Never tell your age. Lie or refuse. These are your choices if you're smart. Two: Do whatever you have to do to look young. Dye your hair. Lose weight. Get a face-lift. Whatever it takes."

"But what about your mind?" pleaded Marie.

"They won't get to know your mind unless you're attractive," said Gosse. Hey, he didn't invent the world. He just knows how to play it.

It's strange, but when I first walked into the room, I noticed Rich, an attractive young man, and Dorothy, a dumpy, conventional older woman. But like the professor who grows more handsome as he speaks, Gosse had begun to sprout feathers. It was Dorothy who became the Buddha.

Before I left, Gosse explained to me that he is happily single and organizes seminars to teach people how to find love because "I enjoy doing it. It's fun and I do it to publicize my book *(Looking For Love in All the Right Places)*. Also, this is how I meet women. I don't *need* to be host, although it is to my advantage. Some women will be attracted to my intellect and my humor." Gosse, the master of meaningless, superficial conversation, also confessed his weakness in looking for love. "I have a problem with intimacy," he said.

"How about you, Dorothy," I asked. "Are you looking for love?"

"Heavens no," she said. "I'm just having a good time. Besides, I believe the more you seek, the less you get."

Town Without Porno

I think it's terrific," said one woman. "I want to cheer," said another. The only porno shop in Berkeley, California, was calling it quits after ten years downtown. The sign in the window, so often a target of the bricks of wrath, proclaimed: GOING OUT OF BUSINESS FINAL SALE. The dusty red, white, and blue banners—the only display of patriotism in town—would soon be coming down. Why?

I'm not sure what I expected when I went in. I suppose some large man with a big cigar and a raspy voice saying, "Sorry, sistah. I don't give no intaviews." Instead what I got was Joe, a twenty-four-year-old junior college student who lives with his mother. Joe does not look well. His eyes are bloodshot—allergies, he explains—and his complexion is sallow. He stands behind an elevated counter where he can monitor the aisles of magazines and books. Below him, in a glass case, are video cassettes with titles like *Hungry Housewife* and *Dear Mr. Plumber*. To his left is a huge case of rubber penises all in Caucasian flesh tones. As I look up at him I can see that his blackened teeth are badly in need of repair.

Joe thought the owner was going out of business because of a rent raise. He speculated that the current rent was about $1,800 a month and said that he believed the property's owner had raised it to $2,500. With $6,000 to $7,000 in gross sales (based on the daily ledger book), that wouldn't leave a big monthly profit after expenses. Joe thought that may have been the reason for the store's going under.

In fact, there are signs that America's $4 billion pornography industry is in trouble. A recent article in *The Wall Street Journal* pointed out that x-rated videos are no longer a growth industry. They attributed the decline to "saturation" in the pornography market and the decision by film studios to release blockbusters as videos. *Raiders of the Lost Ark*, for example, has sold ten times as many cassettes as *Debbie Does Dallas*, the all-time-best-selling sex tape.

Joe explains that he had been out of work for five months before he found this post. His last job was as a sandwich maker. He says what he's learned in the year and a half that he's worked in adult books is "not to trust people." He doubts that the owner was influenced by the constant harassment from feminists who, he said, would come in the store and knock over racks. As recently as two months ago the windows were sprayed with the words *Fight Back*. Bricks, however, no longer fly in since the glass windows were replaced with Plexiglas.

I ask him if he feels there is any truth in the feminist claim (as argued in books like *Pornography: Men Possessing Women*) that items sold in the store exploit women or encourage violence against women. "I agree that in some instances it's exploitative of women, but I don't agree with their tactics," he says. "Actually I think it's exploitative of both men and women. Not the pictures but the words." He points to a number of articles that imply women prefer quantity to quality in men. "Men come in here all the time and ask if we sell penis enlargers."

I ask him about the typical customer and the most popular items. "We get everything from tourists to attorneys," he replies. "No one under eighteen is allowed, but at the beginning of each quarter we get a lot of university students. I'd say it's about eighty percent male, but women do come in for the vibrators." The twenty-five-cent movie booth in the back is the most popular item. Next come the swinger newspapers and the "girlie" magazines. He shows me an inflatable woman "with three orifices" called Love Doll. This sells for $29.95. "I have one customer who bought twenty of them." As we talk several men come up to Joe. With eyes averted and no words exchanged, they hold up a dollar and get four quarters for the movies. Later, before I leave, Joe asks me, "Can you characterize the men you've seen here today?" I said that they seemed older, over fifty, sad, poor, definitely loners. They seemed like the kind of men who are unable to connect with the other people.

Joe says that what really bothers him are the "weirdos"—the men who try to solicit other men in the movie booths, the people who ask for "kiddie porn." "That's illegal and immoral," says Joe. I ask him if his mother knows what he does and Joe says, "She does. She doesn't like it but she knows I need a job."

I tell him I'm going to look around the shop a bit. I remember when I was fourteen and made myself walk down skid row because I wanted to prove that I was tough. I felt that way as I walked among the magazines such as *The Best of Rubber Domination* or the books like *Gestapo Stud Farm* or *Oriental She-Devil* or *Victims of Arab Rapists*. But when I got near those movie booths, I had to run out. It was about the worst thing I've ever smelled.

A few days later I went back in hoping to find the owner. Instead, I was surprised to see a neatly groomed woman in her fifties. It was Lorraine, Joe's mother.

"I just have to tell myself it's a job," she says, explaining that she found the work before Joe. "He was so happy when I told him I found a job in a bookstore because he knows I love to be around books and things. It's rough because I'm an older woman. They can say there's no age discrimination, but there is."

She tells me that before this her last job was "in a Christian organization" but that she couldn't stand the hypocrisy there.

"I'd never been in a place like this before. The ad said 'Mature person for cashiering' and my money was running out. It's an honest business. I mean, they don't do anything illegal. There's no rolling papers; none of that stuff you put in your nose."

For most of her life she's been a housewife and a mother. Ten years ago she got divorced and came to the Bay Area from San Diego. "My primary concern was taking care of my kids. I hadn't worked since before I was married." This job has not been pleasant, she tells me. "One day a young man in a suit came in and tried to steal a magazine. That broke my heart. I've instilled honesty in my son and daughter. They can't stand stealing." I ask how her daughter feels about her job. "She calls me a survivor. It's been hard to get a job because I'm a very shy person. I never look at the stuff here. I just see through it."

Several times she tells me things I am not to print. She complains that the *Daily Cal*, the student paper, interviewed her last year and says they misquoted her. She tells me she's read my articles and likes my writing "except where you had your daughter saying the f-word. I don't think that's right." I explain that I quoted my daughter on the b-word. It was I who used the f-word.

Since we are getting honest here, I decide to ask her what I suspect are painful questions. She tells me the boss has standards. For example, "he doesn't put out any forced bondage magazines." I go to the shelf and get a picture of a nude woman tightly bound and gagged. It is captioned *Punishment by Rape—A Petty Thief's Reward*. "That's just posed," she says. But isn't that forced bondage? I ask. She explains that they "never show penetration while tied up." Next I pick up the book *Mother Loving Boy*, which shows a couple embracing. What about this, I ask. "Incest? It's terrible." But isn't this "just posed?" I press. "That's disgusting," she says, "because it's a child." The child is a boy in his twenties.

We talk about "the feminists" and how scared she is of them. "They're very violent people. The first time I heard them coming up the street, they sounded like students going to a rally. And then they threw garbage in here. They say *this* causes violence, but they're violent. I'm a pacifist."

Lorraine doesn't know what she'll do when the store closes. She's wanted to quit for a long time, but there was never any money saved from the $4.75 an-hour she and Joe make. They're real salt-of-the-earth types, Joe and Lorraine—the kind of people my friends and I cheer for in movies. Lorraine says she will never work in another porno shop again. And she begs me to be careful what I print because she fears the feminists will hurt her.

Ask Ms. Popsych

Dear Ms. Popsych,

Here it is, another Valentine's Day, and I have no sweetheart. No one to send red, lacy hearts to. No one to receive flowers from. No one to share the words *I love you* made out of pure gourmet chocolate, filled with an illegal amount of liqueur.

The problem is, I don't know how to talk to men. I'd as soon board a small plane as start a conversation with a guy. You see, I grew up on a farm with four sisters. My father never spoke to us except to ask, "D'ya do yer chores?" and "Ya got a feller yet?"

Whenever I am with a man, I could just die. I would like to change but I don't know where to begin. I mean, are they interested in baking, sewing, rug shampooing—the things most women in Manhattan talk about?

Can you teach me how to talk to men? And please, don't give me that line about exploring my lesbian potential. Outside of *Cagney and Lacey*, I have no interest in women.

Truly,
Ora Lee Backwards

Dear Ora Lee,

Piece of cake. Next time you see a man that interests you, send a mental arrow to his heart (see my recent paper on this subject, "The Use of Guided Imagery to Snare a Guy," in *The Journal of the American Popsychological Association*). Then you approach him slowly, making sure he is aware of the voom-va-va-voom with which you sling your hips. Once you've got his attention, saunter right up to him, but avoid eye contact (known to be the first warning sign of a ballbuster). When you are within sniffing distance, place your lips close to his ear and whisper in a low, husky voice, "How 'bout those Bears?"

Cordially,
Ms. Popsych

Confidential to Mrs. Weinberger:
Any man who's got to yell "Bombs away!" at a time like that is sick. Stand up to him, honey. Someone's got to stop that maniac.

Dear Ms. Popsych,
I am the last person who ever thought she'd be writing to you, but last month I had a serious midweek crisis.

You see, for the past year I have been a mild-mannered columnist for a weekly paper. It is a strange paper in that it covers everything outside of news, weather, and sports. We had one reporter covering the ego, another on the superego, and I manned the one-woman id desk.

On the morning in question, I looked out the window and saw an old lady in tigerskin rags fishing a Big Mac out of a trash bin. She placed it in the large canvas sack she carried that had the words *Le Bag* written on it. In that instant, a finger in my inner jukebox pushed B-2 and I heard the Beatles singing "I Am the Walrus" and I thought, *deep*. I knew then that someday I would walk some city's streets and people would stare and say, "There goes Le Bag lady. She was once a famous columnist with a big following on a particular block in a midsize city."

During the time I have been writing my column, I have been subjected to a terrifying amount of kindness and acceptance. Outside of the week in which I received two letters—one complaining of my "Jewish angst," the other complaining of my "anti-Semitism"—the politically correct cow town I live in has almost killed me with kindness. There are even people who tell me I should be writing for the *L.A. Times* or *The New York Times* or the *Marina Del Rey Other*. But do these people *know* anybody? No, my friends are these folks who think upwardly mobile is a full-time social services job at twenty-two grand.

Honestly, Ms. Popsych, I wouldn't have written to you if I weren't desperate. I've tried everything else. I went to a shrink. I walked in there and told her all the terrible things that ever happened to me and then I wrote her a check for seventy-five dollars. I came back the next week and started to tell her more terrible things and she interrupted me and said the equivalent of "You better give me the seventy-five dollars right now. Beats hell out of me." Yes, Ms. Popsych, I was rejected by my therapist. This really happened. This is no Woody Allen movie—this is my life.

I tried a new look, but my haircutter failed to show. I considered ODing on the styling mousse right then and there.

I finally tried turning to Gawd, but Gawd didn't answer (or His machine was in the repair shop).

Look, Ms. Popsych, I don't want to spend my old age eating used Big Macs and walking around in a daze singing Roy Orbison songs. I want to go '80s, I just don't know where to get a ticket. Can you help a poor, career spaz like me?

Call me Alice Kahn

Dear Alice Kahn,

What a pathetic pile of bullshit. You have single-mouthedly set the women's movement back fifteen years with that wimp act of yours. If you can't stand the heat, stay out of the sauna.

What you need is so clear and simple that any idiot could tell you what to do. And since you asked me, this idiot will tell you. You need an identity make-over. You need a psychic brain-lift. You need a total fiscal body wrap.

Let's not be shallow about this—a mere stylist will not do. Look at poor Jerry Garcia and what happened to him. He was recently arrested in Golden Gate Park while allegedly free-basing in his BMW with an attaché full of white powder. Now this was obviously a failed attempt to go '80s. He knew it had something to do with BMWs and attaché cases, but nobody told him what to put in them.

On the other hand, look at Jane Fonda. Has she gone '80s, or has she gone '80s? Best of all, she did it without sacrificing her old values (give or take the anticapitalism one). She found something healthy that everybody wanted and marketed it: fitness. It was simply a matter of winning hearts and behinds.

Put that in your BMW and smoke it. Once you stop thinking despair, depression, anxiety, guilt, and start thinking market strategy, target area, growth potential, and venture capital, you'll be on your way.

Cordially,
Ms. Popsych

Confidential to Mrs. Gorbachev:
I agree. If the black silk teddy with the peek-a-boo cups failed to rouse him, he's a goner. I'd take it up with the Politburo. Meantime, you might give him one last chance. Cover yourself with beluga and see if he bites.

Dear Ms. Popsych,
Do you believe in life after birth? I had a baby two years ago and still have not had one moment to myself. Everytime I put the baby down, she cries so I have to pick her back up. When I ask the baby (her name is Tina but we call her Teeny-weeny Sacred One) if she wants anything, she says, "No." When I ask her if I may leave the room, she says, "No." When I ask her for a lav pass, she says, "No." What is wrong? Am I a bad mother?

Concerned,
Momma Stupama

Dear Momma Stup,
There's an old saying, "There's a sucker born every minute"—and we aren't talking about the kid here. The Sacred One has you wrapped around that teeny-weeny finger. She's giving you the business and the finger.

Show her who's boss. Offer her a bribe if she'll let you take a bath alone. If that doesn't work, try getting down on the floor and kicking and screaming. You must set limits for her. When all else fails, wet your pants.

It may also help to remember that this is just one phase in your (and Tina's) life. Things will not always be this way. Someday Tina will mature. She'll change her own diapers and go off to the university (although not necessarily in that order). She'll go out in the world, start her own company, be a success, and refuse to give you a dime in your old age.

Cordially,
Ms. Popsych

Ms. Popsych awaits your letters, your needs, your suffering, and your cash offers. Send your questions and your stock options to: Ms. P., c/o This Newspaper. The first fifteen letter writers will receive a copy of my valuable pamphlet, "The Current Epidemic of Sexually Transmitted Children."

II

The Brie Generation

Where Have
All the Yuppies Gone?
Changing Diapers, Every One . . .

When a highly acclaimed New Orleans-style restaurant in the heart of the nation's definitive yuppie shopping area went bust—lock, stock, and crayfish—in a matter of months, trend-sniffers began to ask why. Are the times, once again, a-changing? (Just as the ancients looked to the stars for answers, we now look at retail sales figures.) One succinct explanation was offered by a person I know. Commenting on the trendy restaurant's demise, she observed, "People are having babies. That means they're eating Mexican or Chinese."

Recently, there's been a rash of articles proclaiming the end of the yuppie life-style (a redundancy in itself). Wags are at work, eager to be first to pronounce the yuppie dead and to perform an autopsy discovering the cause of death as well. Liberals observe a rise in "yuppie guilt" and see in this phenomenon a turning away from the legendary self-centeredness of yuppiedom. They hope this signifies a return to social activism. Didn't the recent mobilization against apartheid on campuses indicate an end to the Brie generation? Even rock stars—the epitome of mega-selfishness—have begun to heed a certain call and donate their alleged talents to programs like Live Aid. Others feel the death of yuppie is a mere whim of fashion. People are tired of the clichés and ready for something new.

Still others point out that the yuppie was always a minority figure, a definable—albeit laughable—type in a generation still struggling to acquire wealth, salaries, and property equal to their elders. Few have actually been willing to identify with this derisive stereotype. Few say it out loud: I'm a yup and I'm proud. Thus, when the end finally comes, few tears will be shed: Don't cry for me, Small Neighborhood Wine Shop. Still, it seems appropriate, to me at least, to give them a decent burial. I've read so many of these yuppie-bashing articles that I've begun to think I've been to the funeral.

Imagine, if you will, a funeral you could die for. The caskets are made of natural redwood and lined with sheets of pearl gray and pale blue—Coastal Fog by Ralph Lauren. The chapel is done in earth tones. In one corner, a string quartet plays wistful renditions of Beatles' "white album" music. The guests are standing around eating tiny vegetables and Tex-Mex spareribs. Some drink the Bordeaux; others don't. The press is positively drooling over the occasion, of course, swigging down fingers of single-malt Scotch and goniffing fistfuls of baguette and cheese. They will spend the service clinging to the Father, Son, and no-Host bar.

Finally, Joe, the Universal Humanist minister, gets up to speak. The guests stop telling horrible jokes and discussing their friends' eating disorders and begin listening attentively. "We gather here today not to praise these yuppies but to bury them," Joe might say. "And not a moment too soon. They've been nothing but an embarrassment to our once morally superior generation. Who amongst us has not had his parents walk into his tastefully furnished yuppitorium and heard them say, 'Ha. Ha. Ha. Whatever happened to "there's more to life than work and possessions?" ' No, we weep not for these rats trapped within the maze of striving and acquiring. Their souls fly not to heaven because they had no souls and none of us believe in any of that stuff anyway.

"Some will ask: What killed Dirk and Bree—that pluperfect

young, professional couple? More significantly, some will walk over to the caskets and look in at the neatly folded suits and ties and say, 'Where are the bodies?' But we speak not of bodily death here, for bodily death is a painful concept none amongst us can bear to consider. Our lives have not prepared us for suffering. We speak here of the only death we with no memory of world war or Depression hunger or low-tech labor can understand—we speak here of trend death. We're talking about our generation. Trend death. The end of an era. The end of the opportunity to relive one's childhood with a credit card and an expense account. Only one question remains. If it is true that yuppies are dead, that the tide is turning away from materialism and toward a New Synthesis, how then, we must always ask ourselves—how then can we profit from this knowledge?"

As Joe speaks the word *profit* a cry rises from the back of the room. At first it is only a tiny "Whaa," but soon it grows to a full crescendo of sobs that seem to say, "Get me out of this place, you mother." It is, of course, a baby.

Were I there, I'd have to leave. The eternal verities combined with the decibel level would surely give me a headache. It's not clear which would be worse, the noise from a screaming baby or the hot air from yet another social critic dancing on the grave of the yuppies. Besides, I'd feel responsible. Had I not contributed mightily to yuppie ridicule with my own trend-sniffing story on the subject four years ago? Did I not hope to build my writing career as the Marcel Proust of North Berkeley, the Tina Turner of premenopausal sarcasm, the Jackie Collins of the East Bay espresso culture by endlessly beating these moribund ponies? Did I not, as recently as one month ago, receive a call from a professor of sociology at Hunter College, saying he was tracing the origins of the word *yuppie* and had found the trail leading to this otherwise undistinguished East Bay housewife? Do I not receive letters asking me if I made up the word and, if I did, why am I not rich and famous?

Let me backtrack for a moment. It's the spring of 1983. I am in the midst of fulfilling a childhood dream. I am writing. In public. For a long time, I felt being a writer was politically incorrect. I should be something socially responsible like a nurse (which I also am). But still, a part of me longs to be naughty, to behave in an ungiving, unnursey manner because, believe me, nobody's that good. So to balance the yin of my nursing job, I start yanging in the alternative press. Some of my patients read it and are shocked. The voice in the paper is not the angel of mercy they think befits a sister of perpetual bedpan-scrubbing. But I persist because I start laboring under the delusion that the Lord is speaking through me via the mysterious route of the dirty joke.

Around this time, I see a cartoon by Roz Chwast in *The New Yorker* that really hits home. It's called "Attack of the Young Professionals." I am, at this time, in a constant state of pissedness because of the instability of my neighborhood, which is clearly becoming more urban. I have lived in the neighborhood—North Berkeley, near Chez Panisse, the nationally famous restaurant credited with spawning "California cuisine"—since 1966, same block since 1968. When I moved in, it was a relatively cheap, empty, quiet area. Like many other neighborhoods, from New York's Columbus Avenue to Chicago's Printing House Row to Los Angeles's Melrose district, it changed.

Actually, my block hasn't changed much and, in fact, despite all the building and development, outside of Chez Panisse and the food stores, very few businesses have succeeded. Still, the place gets dubbed the "gourmet ghetto" and a lot of fancy tourists start parking on my block and looking at me like I'm some kind of quaint local color. So, mature, responsible person that I am, I set out to make fun of them.

Also around this time, the alternative paper for which I write commissions a readership survey. I am shocked by the results. Instead of the scraggly bunch of ex-hippies and die-hard lefties I'd expected, what we've got here are a bunch of mysteriously rich people who travel a lot, exercise a lot, work hard (although not as hard as their East Coast counterparts), and are up to their ears in *life-style*. With the results of this survey before me, I try to create a stereotypical très yup couple named Dirk and Bree and have some fun with Dirk and Bree.

People respond to this story. For months, the paper receives angry letters from humorless yuppies who see themselves being abused by my caricature. One letter comes from a person who gets ahold of the paper's readership survey and says, "Ha-ha. You're just like the people you make fun of." Another writer says, based on this story, "I'm too selfish a person to be a mother." Finally, someone asks plaintively, "How can you make fun of people who eat croissants?"

But ultimately, the joke is on me. The story is reprinted in an L.A. paper and this leads to a call from a big New York publishing connection. Do I want to write the Yuppie Handbook? Do I want a Big Advance? Do I want to be an overnight success? I try to repress my responses to these things and go to work on an outline and sample chapter. Meanwhile, my friend Nina is picking out shoes for me to wear on the Carson show.

Well, let's make a short story shorter: Around the time I started imagining myself riding around in a white BMW with a sunroof and the license plate YUP, the call came from my editors. "Unbeknownst to us, another division of the company signed two women to do the Yuppie Handbook yesterday. Did you make up the word? We think you should consult a lawyer." Was I disappointed? Let's put it this way, I felt like a Gloria Steinem wet dream. I was crushed; it was as if the man of my dreams had left an it-was-swell note on the bed. I had lost my publishing virginity. "Sue them! Sue them!" screamed my well-meaning friends. My only hope was that I'd never hear the word *yuppie* again. Unfortunately, along came Gary Hart and the campaign of '84. Every single article on "yuppies" was sent to me with notes from dear friends saying, "Didn't you make this up? Why don't you sue?"

If I found a roadblock on my path to fame and fortune, others were not so unlucky. A lot of people got richer during the reign of Ronald Reagan, and the stereotype of the wantonly materialistic yuppie began to nag at the generation that really thinks it can have it all—moral indignation and a vacation home. So now we are reading about "yuppie guilt" and how this is disturbing the peace of everyone's investment opportunities. But I, like Reverend Joe, disagree with the theory that the body yupitic is slamming on the moral brakes. There is no doubt in my mind that the death of yuppie was foretold in my story four years ago. The Lord did come down in a dirty joke. The yuppies always contained the seeds of their own destruction. The dream of clean apartments and endless disposable income lies in the shambles of a two-year-old Shiva the Destroyer. The yuppie was hoisted on her own baby.

First, let's get one thing straight. The yuppie was basically a woman. Men have been having it all—indulging themselves, being young and professional—for years. What was new was that gal in the suit and tie and attaché, her bunions bound in Nikes as she commuted home. It was a dream made possible through women's liberation, contraception, and legal abortion. Otherwise, women would still be Nike-less and pregnant and would never know what they were missing, as they had been for generations. So what we are really talking about when we talk about the death of a yuppie is the return of the urge to procreate. Why any woman in her right mind would give up a nine-to-nine job with Bechtel and a styrofoam box of salad in front of the VCR to carry on the race beats hell out of me.

But breed they will, and isn't it obvious? The statistics don't tell the real story. A walk down the street tells the real story, a visit to a singles group tells the real story, an evening at a formerly packed "in" café tells the real story. Is there a gray-haired woman in town who is not with child? After frantically rushing to achieve, in one decade, what had been denied her for all of history, when the noise and music stopped, what our thoroughly modern woman heard was her own biological clock going: cuckoo! cuckoo! Suddenly the young urban professional woman faced the devastating fact that she wouldn't be young forever. Denial is just not something this generation can take standing up. It was a blow. Combine that with the fact that the ratio of men and women begins to change at age thirty-five and that men are encouraged to love younger women and you've got a full-fledged panic to find a sperm donor. I noticed a personals ad recently from a divorced father who specified, "no biological-clock watchers, please."

As if all this weren't bad enough, the once career-oriented woman now faces a barrage of articles, TV reports, and gossip about infertility. I am convinced that what we are seeing is not so much a baby boomlet as a baby panic, inspired (or triggered) as much by the fear of not being able to procreate as by the desire to reproduce one's own miserable existence. The same generation that tried for over a decade to avoid having babies is now willing to go to the high-tech limit to have them regardless of the threat of surgery, multiple births, and subjugating one's sex life entirely to reproduction. How the worm has turned. The risks we once took to control births—pills, devices, operations—we now take to have them.

Don't get me wrong. I certainly understand this desire. Would I trade my two little sweetie pie darlings for a quiet dinner, a clean house, and the possibility of ever sleeping past eight o'clock again? Absolutely not. And no doubt about it, I enjoy seeing all the yuppies give up a life that revolves around satisfying their own needs to one of serving their little angry, crying Buddhas. It's terribly amusing to watch as, one by one, an entire generation becomes humanized by parenthood. It's humbling, to see once arrogant people struggling with such issues as "How do you know when to change the diaper?" And it is, finally, the only way to heal that generation gap that opened when we assumed we were better than our parents, an assumption you can quickly flush when confronted with a child you must raise. Now when I have to meet with some terribly important, intimidating person, I don't imagine him on the toilet. I imagine him toilet training.

If the yuppie was a woman, then certainly the New Parent is a man. Women, of course, have always been the intimates of the diaper. What is really different is the way men are participating in this boomlet. One can hardly walk down the street without seeing a man with a frontpack or a stroller or a free-rider on his shoulders. It's great to see them transforming parenthood as they make business deals in tot lots and devote themselves to turning their daughters into basketball stars and mathematicians. Certainly nothing contributes more to man's respect for woman than when he performs her traditional role of tush scrubber. Similarly, I suspect that women entering such traditionally male bastions as middle-level management have seen the bottom fall out of the glamour of breadwinning. Not that most women will ever want to stay home again. How you gonna keep 'em down on the farm after they've worked for Bechtel? Thus, we have whole new industries developing, profiting from the fact that when this trendy generation become parents, they want to be the best parents money can buy.

This is where it gets scary for me. I can't escape from the thought that having babies is just the latest fad, the "in" thing for the consumer hordes, the coonskin cap and Hula-Hoop and stereo equipment for the '80s. We have always done what the gang did because the herd was just so large. When the pig passed through the python singing, "We Shall Overcome," we all sang. When the pig said, "Stop the bombing," we all said, "Stop the bombing." When the pig came out jogging, we ran in the Bay to Breakers, the annual "fun run" that attracts eighty thousand or more. Now the pig is having piglets and we all just have to have one—or two. Woe to those who do not want them. The social pressure must be unbearable. Even being gay is no excuse. There are regular workshops for gay and lesbian parents. It's not the breeders versus the gays. It's the "listen to my birthing stories," "let's talk about Pampers versus cloth," "where do you stand on private school versus public?"—or be Out Of It. Be pregnant or be square. Of course, you don't have to have children. I mean, it's not for everybody. I think a lot of people are responding to this social pressure by having babies when they ought to do more sensible things like working or getting a tan in Mazatlán or building their wine cellars.

"Should I have a baby?" people wonder. Yes, if you want to be with children. Period. Otherwise, it may be better to maintain number one than to take out your frustrations on Junior. The real sign of the frustrated yuppie parent comes through in the effort to design the perfect childhood. For some, this begins with the search for the ideal sperm donor—a move that can delay birthing indefinitely. A woman I know who works as a midwife said, "What every yuppie woman is really looking for is a hippie carpenter so she can get back to work as soon as possible and he can watch the baby."

The next step in the consumerist approach to parenting is finding the au pair girl. Obviously, in a world that sees nothing bizarre about surrogate mothers bearing children, there should be no hesitation about surrogate mothers raising children. This situation arises from a New Mother mating with an Old Father. They both continue working full-time—frequently not out of absolute economic necessity but because it seems unfair for just one to quit and few employers will accommodate parents. This is especially true for men because what kind of wimp wants to care for baby when he could be working?

One Florida developer, noting that two thirds of the women with school-age children were in the labor force, has designed a town house project around the "child-oriented life-style." In addition to rounded corners on kitchen counters and enclosed patios, the project will include a child-care center providing care during the day, after school, and at night with vans shuttling the kids from school to the center. It may be possible for the parents to go about their business without ever seeing their kids at all. The disquieting aspects of this arrangement are assuaged by the concept of "quality time." Has anybody done a study to determine a baby's position on shlock time?

I don't know how some people can sustain the illusion of what now passes for quality time. In some cases, this comes down to both parents spending an hour or less a day with their infant. Thus, the energy that ought to go into parenting is spent in the search for the ideal au pair and endless rationalizing about the politics of buying someone to raise your baby. (I recently ran into an old friend whom I once knew as a Big Serious Radical. "You know Judy and I lived collectively for many years," he said, "so that's made it easier for us to live with our au pair.")

What is noteworthy about the current baby boom, as *Business Week* magazine points out, is not just that people are having babies but that they are spending a fortune on them. The natural desire to give one's child the best is now combined with a sophisticated marketplace. While 3.6 million births were recorded last year (compared to the 1957 baby boom peak of 4.3 million), the children's products market, now in the $14 billion-a-year range, is expected to reach $20 billion within five years. Money that once went for spas and cuisine and self-help now goes for Apricas and Care Bears and parenting advice. This phenomenal growth is due in part to the fact that older parents, who are further along in their careers, will spend more on their children. It is also because a large number of these older parents are having their first child. The first child not only requires a bigger initial investment, for obvious reasons, but also provides the first opportunity for the parent who's got the consumer habit to transfer his monkey to the back of his baby. Thus we have an increased range of "necessary" baby products from bio-bottoms to designer jeans. We're seeing a rise in cases of layette envy.

This transference of the need to spend from the child within to the offspring has reached its height in yuppie children's department stores and catalogue houses. I visited such a store recently and was disappointed. Really not much grist for the old satire mill there at all—unless you consider the hair salon (with Paddington Bear under the blow-dryer) and the computer section and the catalogue. The clothes are nothing special—the same little Yves Saint Laurent shirts and OshKosh B'Gosh overalls as everyplace else. Outside of the computers, the toys at My Child's Destiny and their display are no big deal to anyone with memories of F.A.O. Schwarz, New York, or Marshall Field, Chicago. What did amuse me was the following conversation between two mothers who were pushing their babies in those strollers that also convert to cribs, car seats, and yachts.

Mom A: I just hope he plays with all these rattles I bought him.

Mom B: If he doesn't, he can always take them with him to Princeton.

The blatant snob appeal at this store comes through the catalogue—a kind of Sharper Image for parenting. There is a family portrait of the owners (son in tie and jacket, daughter neat as a pin) above the message: "We look for natural fibers, top design, and excellent wearability in our clothing. Our toy selections must stimulate creativity and provide extended play value. The books we choose must be fun or educational or both and be bias-free. As always, we guarantee all our products to be the best in their area."

How will the parents of this top-of-the-line child cope when confronted with that wild rebelliousness that is the birthright of every decent human being? Perhaps, as long as there is only one child and two parents, this orderly view of childhood can be sustained. But my experience is that once the suckers start thinking, "We've done so well with one, why not go for two?"—this is when the party is really over. Once a yuppie suffers from such delusions of competence that she has two kids, she's finished as a yuppie. The dream is over. She can turn in her bow tie at the gate. It's one big sacrifice from here to social security. But that, after all, is why we've got to have those babies. Who else will pay into the system?

As a seasoned yupologist, I personally do not think we've seen the last of the yuppie life-style. What I see happening is a greater rift between the two elements in the baby-boom generation— those with kids and those without. We've already seen some of this as people with children increasingly are falling below the poverty line. We also see it in development issues. People without children tend to favor more nightlife and adult-oriented businesses like bars, restaurants, and health clubs, while those raising families want peace and quiet and parks and schools. This conflict of interest was illustrated recently at one of my favorite restaurants. What I saw there summed up the urban struggle: parents versus singles.

My husband and I were there because we were lucky enough to land a baby-sitter. It's one of those crowded little places that we've learned through experience is not a good place to bring the kids. (It only took a few tries to realize it's the rare child who loves calamari salad.) We were seated within deodorant-sniffing range of another couple who were such central-casting yups I thought I must have made them up. (Dirk and Bree live, I thought.) He kept talking about how many "reps" he did at his health club and his problems trying to "refi" some property. At one point, she actually took out photos of her time-share. He said he didn't like the design of the fireplace. "Well, I do," she said.

They discussed the problems of trying to find a one-bedroom in the city for under eight hundred a month. He talked about architecture and whether the Jane Fonda tapes sell in small towns in the Midwest. "I'd like to see the stats on that," he said. She said, "I've got a terrific travel opportunity if I want to take it." While I'm choking on my tortellini and straining to memorize this conversation, I notice that at the next table two couples have been seated, one with a new baby. My husband and I are somewhat amused to see them struggling to carry on as if nothing has changed in their life. We recall a point at which we cherished such illusions: No big deal—like a cat in diapers. The baby, of course, will have none of the crowded, hot restaurant and the loud, wine-drenched conversations, and commences screaming. The father tries to cheer the baby—pacifier, bouncing, burping. He gets nowhere and the baby continues wailing. Finally, we see the father make a diaper check by discreetly sticking his finger in the baby's suit—a move that invites either reassurance or social isolation. The baby is clean but still crying. Frustrated, the father hands the child to the mother. She tries nursing, but nursing won't work. The child is now doing a full Pavarotti.

The yuppie couple next to us can no longer continue their conversation. They both turn around in unison and glare at the noisy baby. The woman says to the man loud enough for the frazzled parents to hear, "Couldn't she afford a baby-sitter?"

While every newspaper has run a gleeful death-of-yuppie story, none has really tied it to the baby boomlet and the dichotomy it creates for what has been a notably herd-oriented generation. It will be interesting to see how the politics of this split plays itself out. There is clearly a conflict of interest between the couple seeking adult nightlife and the family wanting someplace to go out to together. One wonders: As all the shell-shocked new parents settle down to the long, thankless task of turning their babies into civilized creatures, will we see this group return to the socially conscious mentality associated with the '60s, or will they retreat to a more immediate concern for protecting family and home? Will the new parents become more involved in global issues or, too exhausted for meetings, take on an I-gave-at-home attitude? Will those who choose not to have children, or who refuse to have them in the absence of fiscal and emotional support, turn their surplus energies to nourishing mankind? Or, finding themselves increasingly isolated from the procreative mainstream, will they become more self-absorbed in an urban, adults-only world?

It's clearly too early to say what will happen now that one trend is nearly dead and another is in the delivery room. But I know what Reverend Joe would say if he were here. He'd say, "If there is a God, he'd invest in Day Care-Я-Us."

Jog Is Dead

Stress . . . can't live with it, can't live without it. But for a while I thought I could outrun it. I followed the advice of my friend Don the exercise king. Don convinced me that we had to make up for the lack of physical labor our modern bodies still craved through exercise. Jog four to six miles a day. That, I thought, would keep the beast at bay.

You have to understand that I had been stone sedentary since grammar school when the intimidatingly agile black girls forced me into a life of spazdom. In retrospect, I wonder if the main disadvantage of a ghetto education was not that I didn't become a doctor or a lawyer but that I didn't become a jock. To the girl who was chosen last for teams, jogging was the perfect sport. For ten years I ran with the dogged determination and the unskilled raw stamina of the mental athlete.

So where did I end up for my trouble? I ended up with the heart and lungs of a twelve-year-old, the mind of an adolescent (which I've always had), the insatiable lust of a forty-year-old woman, and the big toe of a moribund eighty-year-old. The toe! Who would have guessed the toe would do me in? Ten years of devotion to the sweet pain of jogging and I end up with a stress fracture. Stress fracture! The irony of it, the ignominy of it, the incredible pain in the foot.

According to my foot man, Dr. Machete, ace podiatrist, I had to stop running, at least temporarily. Stop running—what was left? Working, eating, sex, reading, conversation, mental masturbation, masturbation masturbation—in short, nothing. We're talking major tragedy here. Well, maybe there was a part of me that sort of wanted to stop, that was sick to death of the route, the deep breathing, the need to stay sober until it was over, the yo-yo-heave-ho of right foot then left. This was probably the part of me that my friend Mark saw when he confessed, "The last few times I saw you running across Shattuck Avenue, you looked near death."

The truth is, I was afraid to stop. I was afraid that if I did I'd gain weight, I'd feel depressed, I'd pick on my loved ones, I'd be boring. So I stopped. What happened? I gained weight. I felt depressed. I tormented my loved ones. I was so boring, I couldn't stand to listen to myself for more than fifteen minutes without saying: you're boring, you're fat, you're nothing since you stopped jogging. Walking, I continued to do. I could walk just fine. I could walk like a man. Still, I longed to run like a bitch.

Since I was a lost cause, a hopeless downer, a washed-up jogger, a pastured nag, I decided to drown my sorrows in food. I know there are a lot of women who think it's politically incorrect to complain about being a little fat. It's a capitulation to Hefner. It's a sign of manipulation. It's an indication of lack of acceptance of the almighty Self. But, fat friends, forgive me—I despised every new bit of flab I was acquiring. The more I saw, the more I ate. And I wasn't just eating granola, you know. I was into deepest, darkest junk food; jelly beans, mint Oreos, bread whiter than Nancy Reagan's *tuchus*. I was like a bulimic who refused to puke.

Then one day I dragged my expanding self to a used-bike store and decided to cast my fate to traffic. I could give you a hundred reasons for not riding a bike: It isn't aerobic enough; children do it; it forces you into an intimate relationship and a compromising position with a machine; I don't have the little black suit; every time you blow the horn another angel enters heaven; you get numb Down There; unless you get a four-hundred-dollar mountain bike it's not hip; you can lose your cherry; people get killed doing it; etc. etc. I thought: You call these reasons? The stress of life was killing me. The separation anxiety from jogging was killing me. The depression was too depressing. So I started pedaling for success.

I'll tell you a secret about riding a bike. It's fun. Way more fun than jogging, although I think you have to ride for about an hour and a half even to approach the exhaustion of a half-hour run. Still, there is something about the feel of the wind that you get on a bike—and the sound of the whirling in your ears—that's really fun. The problem, however, with riding a bike in the city is that right around the time you're really enjoying it and are relaxing and getting high on the wind, you're probably close to your death. Even if you ride a bike like I've been doing—strictly recreation, no destination, seeking the least busy streets—without constant vigilance you will be squashed by that stalking monster, the automobile. Since I started riding a bike, I view automobiles as much more menacing than I ever did as a pedestrian. There's not just the *risk* of an accident. They really are out to kill you!

My route takes me through Ohlone Park—a nice little urban park—and then on the BART bike path. (Unlike the old subways in the old countries back East, your modern Bay Area Rapid Transit includes a bike path below the elevated tracks.) Riding along here, you risk your life only at intermittent intervals and can skip the murderous curbside car-door openings that loom like constant life-ectomies to the biker. You can actually space out for long stretches as your pumping legs magically take you into wondrously normal Albany, the all-American town. Then it's on the backroads of suburban El Cerrito, where upwardly mobile Asians and Indians live in spotless stucco apartments. You even see a few foundries and lumberyards and creeks and the rear end of the El

Cerrito Plaza, an actual mall, for your labors. You can thrill to the ever-present graffiti. I wonder if the mysterious Barbara has figured out which spray-can poet has devoted his life to letting the world know, "Barbara, I want your body."

I'm still new to this bike business. I have mastered minor breakdowns that I regard as major victories. I hate machines. I tend to destroy them. I stick spoons in blender blades and mangle forks in Mixmasters and do things to automobiles too obscene to mention in front of decent people. I nearly panicked when the chain came off the bike, miles from my home and not a penny in my pocket. But I just calmed down and said: What would some studly biker do at a time like this? And you know what I did? I picked up the chain with my bare hands and put it back on the sprocket. And pretty soon I was on the road again—going places that I'd never been!

There are only two hard-and-fast rules I've evolved for riding a bike. One is: Drive defensively. And by this I mean *real* defensively, which means that you regard every driver of every automobile as a homicidal maniac—especially little Alfa Romeos. Those people will squash you like a dead skunk in a flash. You'll be just another black-and-white dotted line if they have their way. My other rule is: Never drive under the influence. I tried that once. I had merely had a little late afternoon tête-à-tête with Mr. Remy and Mr. Martin—just a snifter, mind you, but enough to encourage me to try a look-Ma-no-hands. I still have a lovely chartreuse-and-amber tattoo on my leg where I collided with the parked van. If you drink, don't do bike tricks.

In addition to the bike I've also cast my fate to the waters. I finally made it to the lap pool and now go an occasional twenty or thirty rounds with the other lapdogs. It's fun, it's low-calorie, and you're too busy to worry about whether the other people are peeing in the pool. Swimming is a special thrill. My parents were so against it, I grew up thinking there was a commandment in the Old Testament against swimming: Thou shalt not get thy hair wet. I also grew up in the '50s, when you could get polio just by looking at a swimming pool. Thus, taking the plunge has an added kick of breaking with the taboos of my childhood. The very idea of going to a swimming pool regularly is mind-blowing. Where do I think I am—California? Swimming also is more fun than jogging except for the part about getting in and out.

But jogging is still my first love, and as soon as Dr. Machete dropped the knife and said, "Okay, but stretch first and do no more than twenty minutes at the track," I was back. It's not my whole life anymore, though. I would have stayed in the jogging rut forever, grimly determined, dry, unwheeling, had I not been forced to experiment. Now I have a choice. Or, I can do a combo —one from column A and two from column B. This week I finally did it all in one day. I ran six laps, then biked five miles, then swam twenty laps. All in one day. Little me, the one who never got chosen for the team, the girl who, had she gone to a white grammar school, might have been a hoop queen instead of a basket case. So what if I'm not the Iron Man? At least I'm in the running for the Kleenex Woman.

Lookin' At You, Kid

People dress for two reasons—sex and success. Those seeking neither merely get dressed. But since we all have mirrors, I suspect that there is motive if not method in even the most ardent schlep who insists, "I couldn't care less about the way I look."

When we talk image this year, we're inevitably talking Don Johnson and Cybill Shepherd. Johnson, also known as "the white guy on *Miami Vice,*" popularized the tropical gangster look with his parachute pants, pastel T-shirts, white linen jackets, and slipper shoes worn without socks. The fact that he is a cop never seems to bother anyone as he performs his bust-dances set against blue skies, deco buildings, and pulsating music, to a climax in the cry: "Freeze! Miami Vice." The traditional "sissyness" of Johnson's clothes is balanced by the "stubble look" (a carefully contrived five o'clock shadow) and the decidedly masculine fashion statement of a pointed gun. Très chic. Très now. Très Rambo.

Shepherd represents the trend among businesswomen, toward refeminization. If men's clothes can be more feminine, then why do women have to wear ties? Enter Cybill Shepherd, blondie blonde, former cover girl now worried money manager in the TV series *Moonlighting.* On the show Shepherd presents a new image that can only be described as yuppie slut. You take your basic business suit and slit it up the front so that every step you take reveals not only your business but, practically, your *pupik*. Then you take that silk blouse and unbutton most of the buttons. Through this process we get to see the amazing Shepherd cleavage, which seems to start at her chin. Some feel that a businesswoman who adopts a modified Shepherd is signaling that she has reached her level of incompetence and is no longer movin' on up, a process known as "fluffing out."

If this is TV's idea of dressing for success, why do we see so few Johnson and Shepherds wanna-bes walking our streets? More likely, men are apt to demonstrate their wild-and-craziness through fashion denial or the daring fashion statement of a yellow tie. Why the color yellow? I can only refer back to the basic fashion rule of the '50s: Only fairies wear yellow on Thursday. Yellow is slightly fem and is about as far as most men will go to indicate a softening of their position.

For women, the main fashion concession seems to be the addition of padded shoulders, which creates the appearance of perpetual insouciance, a spasmodic posture of shrugging one's shoulders at the world. But much more incredible trends are descending from Paris. There's talk of hip pads and buttocks pads! Once they start talking thigh pads, we can put those suction lipectomy guys out of business. Then every inheritance *will* be a blessing.

If dressing to please the boss is what characterizes adult life, then it is only among the youth that we can observe fashion as pure creative expression and in its traditional role, that of courtship plumage. That's why I found myself among the unnaked and the undead: high noon at Berkeley High, a school much celebrated for being "multi" everything—multiethnic, multisexual, multigoofy.

Walking into the center of the campus lunchtime crowd, the energy was so high you almost felt in danger, as if lightning could strike. The group formed a sea of black and bleached blonde and tight ankles and long earrings and shirttails dangling. I thought of Yeats's "Among School Children." I looked for teenagers I knew, saw a few, thought of approaching, but held back feeling like a creep: a forty-one-year-old smiling public woman.

I sat down on the steps of the Community Theater and started taking notes, when a young man looked at me and said, "Should I act weirder?"

This would be Craig Wichner a junior, dressed as nondescriptly as possible: plain Levis (neither new, torn, nor faded), a round-neck sweater, white leather jogging shoes, short hair, no jewelry. "My style is the nonstyle," he explained.

Wichner, whose nonstyle look probably represents the most popular fashion image at Berkeley High, then went on to fill me in on the turf arrangements and the style groups in the schoolyard. I've yet to meet a more charming and engaging informant.

He pointed out the trendies, who sit on one section of the theater steps. "Those are the jocks and the princesses, the rich kids, the young, *young* upwardly mobile preppies," characterized by baggy pants with rolled-up cuffs, shirts hanging out ("nothing is tucked in"), baggy sweatshirts, and sometimes—on girls—very tight pants or leggings that are like tights with stirrups. Farther along the steps were the punks or rockers in mostly black with bleached blond or multicolored hair on boys and girls alike. To their left sat the heavy metalers with very long hair, leather studded jackets, and Ozzy Osbourne shirts. Another group identified by Wichner was what he called the European punks. "These are guys who go after teenyboppers who like Duran Duran and Thomas Dolby. They're more stylized and wear hats with their bangs fluffed out and makeup."

Wichner explained that neither makeup, jewelry, nor anything previously considered feminine signaled that a boy was gay. "Style is a form of self-expression," he said, and cautioned, "You can't really call somebody a trendie or a rocker because they might change from day to day or they might be in-between."

In addition to acknowledging the raza turf toward the front of the high school, Wichner described another area as belonging to what he called "the culturally black" students. "They're into looking sharp, good clothes, expensive clothes. This year it's Gucci sweaters and Gucci shirts." Outside of these two exclusive groups, which Wichner said sometimes made him feel "excluded," the majority of the campus sat in well-integrated groups of four or more. I noticed the red anti-apartheid ribbons all over the place and my informant told me that the trendies favor the blue ribbons. "Blue ribbons mean they gave supplies to Nicaragua. The trendies are into that as well as the *We Are the World* album." I suppose it's only in Berkeley that you include your favorite revolution as part of your fashion statement.

We were joined by Aaron Brownson, another nonstyler, a senior. He spoke with slight contempt of the trendies as "kids from the hills, kids in hundred-dollar jackets." Thus I was a bit surprised when I asked him what look would attract him in a girl. "Trendy looks nice to me," he said. "When I see a punk rocker I think maybe she's a troubled girl." He pointed to a boy in black with bleached blond hair and said, "That's cool but there's probably some pain in his life."

Slowly but surely more friends of Wichner's joined us. Girls tended to give him a big hello and walk away. Boys wanted to find out what the strange lady was doing. Matthew McCully, also a junior, was wearing a blazer and bell-bottom trousers. Virtually every kid I know in Berkeley despises the hippie look, so I asked McCully if the bells were deliberate. He insisted, "I don't care what they're wearing as long as they're a nice person." Remember when you could still say stuff like that with a straight face?

Jay Bryon explained his brown leather jacket this way: "I tried to get a heavy metal jacket [i.e., black, studded], but my parents wouldn't go for it. I have a taste for thrash metal." "Was that trash metal?" I asked, revealing my prejudices. "*No, thrash* metal; but I could fit in with the trendies. I like violent bands like Exodus. Ozzy Osbourne's just a pacifier, a poser. . . ." And this kid, like the rest, was as sweet as they come, a perfect son, a great boyfriend.

Finally, we were joined by Noah Landis, whose bleached blond Mohawk was pushed down under a backward black cap. All the others had pointed him out as an outrageous dresser, a true punk rocker. Landis, too, made a pious speech about how dress means nothing. A terribly sweet girl named Katherine Falk joined us and added, "Dress means nothing. It doesn't say anything about your personality." But she allowed that there are some fashions she would like to wear, like the leggings, but she doesn't feel she has the figure for it. Like most women, she knows fashion is an expression of how much you want to show off or hide your body.

Later, I discussed my conversation with the boys with my friends Amy and Jenny, a sophomore and senior at Berkeley High, and the first humans I have watched grow up. I've seen them turn from little babies into blond bombshells. Smart, funny, and a little outrageous, Jenny and Amy are pure one hundred percent Berkeley homegrown.

Here's what Amy has to say about fashion: "Clothes at Berkeley High are the ugliest I've seen since the 1970s disco phase. I haven't bought anything new because they're so ugly. There're two styles: preppie and boring. Kids wear loud, obnoxious things I used to wear for a joke, like paisleys. They're serious. . . ." Although she wouldn't say what she liked in boys, she said, "I'll tell you what I find obnoxious. I hate the 'queer look' boys have— teased-up hair, makeup, jewelry. The guy has more makeup than I do. Why do they do it? Because stupid girls like it. They'll tell their boyfriend, 'Oh, you look so cute in eyeliner.' As for adults, 'I guess I don't look at older people's clothes. They're ugly in different ways. They're business ladies and stuff.' "

Jenny observed that one trend this year seemed to be a merging of styles among black and white students. "I've read a lot about music styles merging, about artists like Prince," she said. "What's a black record anyway? Do they write down people's race when they buy a record? But the black girls used to laugh at things me and my friends wore that they're now wearing. Things like stuff that doesn't match, weirder looks." Others, too, are adopting the styles that Jenny liked as an avant-garde sixth-grader. "People that used to make fun of ripped jeans are now wearing them. White trendies are now bleaching their hair. Preppie guys have these stupid-looking flattops that they spike up. When I was doing a report on the history of fashion, about how women shed corsets to be liberated, then started wearing girdles because they were liberated, I read somewhere, 'There's nothing you can wear to be different that the media can't make into fashion.' " She says of the trends at Berkeley High, "It's cool to be different, but since everybody's different it all looks the same."

I was feeling terrific about Berkeley High. What an interesting group of sophisticated but thoughtful people are here. If they mirror us, then we're not as bad off as I sometimes fear we are.

The reason I finally left the Berkeley High campus was that some men with walkie-talkies, the supervisors, shooed everyone back to class. The electric force-field teeming with hormonally determined life was quickly transformed into a garbage pit of milk cartons and chip bags. A janitor started raking it up. Seagulls and pigeons descended.

I approached one supervisor, a natty gent in a trenchcoat and hunting cap, thinking I'd interview him on fashion. But while I was introducing myself another supervisor rushed up and said, "We caught two white guys on the roof. They had short hair, black gym shoes, white T-shirts, and another guy . . ." I couldn't hear his description of the other guy. I'd spent the day talking about clothes so naturally I asked, "What was he wearing?"

"Wearing?" asked the supervisor, looking at me strangely. "He wasn't wearing nothing. He was naked. And masturbating."

I buttoned my drab tweed jacket and went home.

Adventures
in the Book Trade

Almost exactly sixty-five years to the day since my mother, the late Idell Aronovitch Nelson, got lost at a fish market in Danzig, there I was at the Moscone Convention Center in San Francisco, lost in the marketplace of ideas. But surely a pile of Polish carp could not have been more engrossing than the eighty-fifth annual convention of the American Booksellers Association (abbreviated as the ABA). As I wandered aimlessly among the twenty thousand assembled literati, diskerati, and kiddie litterers, I could not help asking myself the obvious pompous intellectual question: What does this tell us about ourselves? To which I quickly responded: Who cares? Grab a shopping bag and fill it up with free stuff.

This was, after all, a trade show with over three thousand booths lining the midway, each outdoing the other in good old American hustle. "Step right up and get your Delmore Schwartz and James Joyce here. Meet distinguished psychologist and noted Rabbi Dr. Saul Landau . . ." Titles grabbed you: *Sexual Desire: Its Meaning and Its Goal; I Wish My Parents Understood: A Report on the Teenage Female; Megatraumas; A Woman and Her Self-Esteem . . .*

Did you miss John Z. De Lorean in person? No problem, catch his videotape.

It was a carnival atmosphere—my favorite. As soon as I entered I was hugged by an eight-foot-tall bunny named "Hartley." "What sex are you, Hartley? How much do they pay you to degrade yourself?" Hartley wasn't talking. I heard a woman from *Publishers Weekly* scream out, "My God. There's a woman in a mouse uniform." Next my hand was grabbed by a giant yellow creature—it was a Fird, half fish, half bird. I was accosted by a "Rabbi" Moonlight from Point Arena, California, who was hawking his book, *The Brand New Testament*, available from Joydeism Press and featuring The Ten Suggestions. Then, there was Zippy the Pinhead in the simulated flesh passing out "Are We Having Fun Yet?" buttons. Two central-casting tweedies at the Harvard University Press booth were seen giggling at him. "I saw that, Harvard, and I'm going to tell," I said. They giggled some more beneath their old school ties.

There were Manhattan mega-publishing czars in tailoring so elegant, I almost swooned. They had, however, those tormented faces that told you that while they were dressed for success they were also paying for it with hemorrhoids that often lie too deep for tears. There were Wellesley College types ready to prove they could be as vicious as any man. There were booksellers from Utah in buckskin. There were ladies from Minnesota wheeling their shopping bags of freebies on suitcase carts. It was like supermarket sweepstakes. In the morning, two hundred copies of Colleen McCullough's new book would be offered to Moe's Used Books.

A superficial impression (am I capable of any other?) might lead one to believe that the majority of readers in this country are preschool children, gay communists, or lobotomized housewives. At least, these seem to emerge as the big markets, judging from the number of titles being pitched to them. There were hundreds of romance books all with cover paintings of ladies having their Victorian gowns ripped off by naked men. (Think of the scandal if just one of those men were black.) One romance publisher had a huge booth with pink and lace walls and live harp music. But this didn't approach the hype from the preschool publishers out to grab the bucks from baby-boomers who are eager to spend for their little one-and-only. I'm sure we'll be seeing *How to Teach Your Baby Advanced Calculus* soon. I was standing looking at the great kid math books when I saw someone I knew, who advised, "Just go ahead and take them . . . they're free." Soon a rep from Golden Books was grabbing *Getting Ready to Add* out of my hands. "You didn't move quickly enough," my acquaintance snickered. The rep, however, did give me their free sample, which turned out to be an adorable kindergarten activity book on how to thwart molesters.

Left-wing interests were well represented with new books on Central America, although publishers had failed to anticipate the interest in South Africa. The strength of the gay market was indicated in a special convention workshop called "Using a Gay/ Lesbian Section to Increase Store Sales." The Christian market was also looking good, although a little heavy on the records and diskettes. I talked to the Word Publishing rep who was there selling the patriotic songs of Pat Boone. "You know Pat Boone?" he asked me.

"Yes," I confessed, "but I'm really more of an Elvis fan. So, you're from Waco, Texas?" (I considered it the height of good manners that I did not pronounce it *Wacko.*)

"Waco's a great place to raise kids," he told me. Then he added, "But I was born in New York, so I know about *life-style.* . . ."

Perhaps next year's theme ought to be "Why don't straights and Christians read?" This year's theme was "Toward a reading society," which even the ABA director observed was at odds with the slogan "A nation of readers." Judging from all the new books and articles about illiteracy, we've got a long way to go. However, nobody outside of the Couch Potatoes (those TV devotees) questions the idea that reading is inherently good; even those Americans who don't read probably share that assumption. Let's put it his way: We all agree, regardless of what we do, that reading a book is better than, say, watching a cassette of *Stuffing It Down Debbie's Throat*. However, when you see books as they are here—marketed like any other product—their inherent superiority to other forms of entertainment is not so obvious, except that books are a lot cheaper. Jean Day, of Small Press Distribution, noted, "When people come by and pick up our catalogue, I say, 'We only have literature . . .' and then they put it down."

At one point I found myself in the midst of the Marin County literati—both of them. He slapped a colored dot on my hand, a "Stressdot," which was like getting your emotional colors done. Mine was olive—"on edge." She handed me *The Breast Pocket Calendar*, a tiny calendar with photos of breasts, and her card. "Who are you?" she asked.

Having overused the I'm-nobody-who-are-you line, I said, "An author."

"Well," he said without a moment's hesitation, "why don't we get together and discuss a project?"

"Are you networking me?" I asked.

"I'd like to network you," she said flatly. "Can we get together, have lunch, and brainstorm?"

Was this how the smalltimers hustled? Over at Simon and Shyster they had a whole section labeled "Subsidiary Rights" and those folks were dealing. Some guy with a Lorimar Productions tag was saying to someone, "So I'll take your card and you'll take my card and maybe something will come of it." Remember Woody Allen's idea of California? "Well, you take a meeting with him and I'll take a meeting with you. . . . Right now it's only a notion, but I think we can get money to make it a concept and later turn it into an idea."

Having had my fill of the serious big publishers, I headed toward the low-rent district, the small press area. First I obtained the autograph of the author of *Biceps and Buns*, rushing over to meet Mr. B&B at his booth. "I only posed above the waist," he insisted.

I found Lily Pond, the ex-hippie turned wholesome eroticist, displaying her journal *Yellow Silk* at the Down There Press booth. Down There was holding a drawing for a vibrator, which I held up and interviewed people with. Everyone answered my questions politely. Seconds later, none other than "Scoop" Nisker, Mr. Question Man himself, was shoving his vibrator (you don't think it's really a microphone?) in my face and interviewing me for his radio show. Off the air, we discussed the major issues that people talk about at these literary events: Where's the free food? Outside of an ice cream sandwich (my major score) and a glass of Chablis from Grove Press, it was slim pickings. I looked above the hedge of daisies at the Sunset booth, but there wasn't even a lousy pasta salad. I went out of my way to meet Tom and Marilyn Bagel, authors of *The Bagels' Bagel Book* ("a no-holes-barred account . . ."), but I missed the free lunch. I did, however, follow Julia Child around, thinking she'd find the good stuff. Instead, she became intrigued with a video cassette of *Classical Cooking Made Easy*.

Still in the small-press area, I met author Ed Rosenthal and I'll bet you can't name his million-copy-selling book. Ed is the author of *The Marijuana Grower's Guide* and has just published a sequel, *The Marijuana Grower's Handbook*, with his own newly formed Quick American Publishing Company. He is also a columnist for *High Times* magazine—the Ask Ed column. I asked Ed the secret to his success. "I was deeply inspired by Kahlil Gibran, who taught me that you don't need a lotta words to fill a page."

Carrying those powerful words with me, and two full shopping bags of crap, I headed to the BART (Bay Area Rapid Transit) station, still happy to be Little Ms. Nobody from the hinterlands and not the best-selling authoress of *Blood Suck Wedding* and two hundred other stomach-wrenching novels. Once home, I gave daughter Hannah the balloon that said, "Psssst," the Flavor Bears scratch-and-sniff button, and the "I (Heart) Biceps and Buns" button, Shari Lewis's *One Minute Stories* for busy parents, and a *Barbie Magazine*. Daughter Emma, the only one in the family with taste, declined anything except a University of Arizona Press poster of a cactus fruit being cut open and a "Woman of the Future" button. Husband Eddie accepted a free *Playboy*, the *Granville Market Letter*, and *The Times Literary Supplement*, but refused a "Color Me Macho" button. That left me with *The Chico Restaurant Guide*, one "Be Competent: The Way to Happiness" bumper sticker, the magazine *Today's Christian Woman*, a "Go for It" balloon, a paper plate that said *"Eat to Win* Now on Video," and a "Winning Through Integrity" button.

I didn't get to the autograph area—the lines were too long. But I can dream. Maybe next year I'll be there alongside Jonathan Kozol *(Illiterate America)*, Mr. T *(Mr. T)*, Collier and Horowitz *(The Kennedys)*, Celeste De Blasis *(Wild Swan)*, Rosemary Curb and Nancy Manahan *(Lesbian Nuns)*; Gayle Peterson *(Pregnancy as Healing*, vol. 2), Paul Krassner *(Best of the Realist)*, Joannie Greggins *(High Energy Aerobics)*, Elmore Leonard *(Glitz)*, and Marco *(It'll Grow Back)*. Is this democracy or what? In Poland today you can only get one or two fish—if you're lucky. As that great literary character Sonny Corleone once said, "I love this country." Well, he said it in the movie. I never read the book.

The Momist Manifesto

Recently I was a minor participant in a unique event. Bananas, a pioneering parent support organization, and the local First Presbyterian Church held "Parenting Twenty-five Hours a Day: A Special Event for Families." It was my job to walk around during the lunch hour interviewing members of *the* oppressed group of the '80s—parents.

The entire conference right down to professional child care was free. It included workshops on child *and* parent development, being a single parent, a new parent, a stepparent; one entitled "Dual (Not Duel) Careers," and, my favorite, one on "Setting Limits (Formerly Known as Discipline)." You can't even mention the d-word anymore.

At lunchtime, I walked around with Judy Calder, a registered nurse who works full-time with the Bananas organization. Calder operated the video equipment while I did the interviews. I think Bananas hoped I would provide some spritely entertainment for their video files, a little gal-in-the-street zaniness with those lovable, laughable parents. Instead, as Calder observed, "the interviews were really poignant."

Why is parenting in the '80s such serious business? Why do we find a role that dates back to Adam and Eve so stressful? There are lots of answers, lots of places to put the blame, but I think the major reason is because parents are trying so hard to do the job well. Everyone I know, including myself, is obsessed with trying to be something called "a good parent." This is a particularly elusive concept since the desired outcome is so unclear. What is the goal? A moral child? A successful child? A happy child? A child who loves you? An independent child? All of the above?

My impression of the parents I interviewed was that most of them were already in the top ten percentile of parenting. Almost by definition, anyone who would spend their entire Saturday focusing on how to be a better parent is already half there. Other parents were probably spending their time doing chores, fighting with their kids, escaping from their kids, or, rarely, having fun with their kids.

Many of the people at the conference were child-care workers in addition to being parents. They discussed the problem of being listened to by their client kids while being rebuffed by their own kids. Parents of teens talked about the pain of being rejected (except, of course, when needed as a funding agent) by their youngsters, who are choosing the support of their peer group. Some parents talked about the problems of balancing career and family.

One woman discussed her decision to leave her job as an executive at AT&T to stay home. "I decided I was paying someone to do my job while I was at my other job," she said. I thought of how hard, as a black woman, the road to her executive position must have been, and what a difficult choice that must have been. Her comment will surely strike at the guilt feelings of other mothers who are afraid to leave their jobs because of uncertainty over whether they could come back, because they can't afford it, or because they simply can't stand to be home with the children full-time. Some fathers may feel this conflict, too, but they have not experienced the rapidly changing expectations that women have. While 46 percent of American women were housewives in 1960, today that number has been cut to 20 percent. All indications are that this percentage will continue to decline. But it doesn't change the fact that these mothers still grew up in a world where women were expected to stay home and raise the children.

A stepfather talked to me about the importance of being patient in winning the love of his three-year-old stepchild. He observed that he had no more right to expect the child's love than any stranger on the street. But he said after a year of patient attention, the child (whose natural father was named Carl) came up to him one day and said, "You're my Carl."

Two couples with babies less than a year old talked about how the youngsters had changed their relationships. In both cases, the women stayed at home. One man talked about his difficulty with coming home tired from work and finding the wife at the door passing him the baby and saying the equivalent of "You take the little bugger, I'm getting out."

All these problems seemed familiar, some I've experienced, some I've only heard about. What struck me was that regardless of class, style, or any other variable, I can always empathize with that struggle to raise a child well.

It is a struggle compounded by the fact that in the modern family, the child has replaced the father as house tyrant. We all scurry around trying to meet that child's needs, trying not to cross him. How many times have you seen a mother (and that mother might have been me) standing in the supermarket presenting a reasonable list of alternatives to an unreasonable screaming little person who stood there shouting, "No, no, no, no"?

Discipline is a real thorn in the side of those who spent their formative years rejecting all forms of discipline and control. We fear damaging or repressing our children as we complained our parents did to us. In the context of a "question authority" community, it becomes particularly difficult to set limits for our children. That's why we feel such gratitude for anyone who seems to be on our side, anyone who understands that discipline is not the equivalent of child abuse.

Recently a woman asked me, in a somewhat confrontational manner, "What are your politics?" The whole presentation of this question had a '60s milieu about it, and I immediately fell into a '60s response, saying somewhat sheepishly and guiltily, "I used to have politics, but I haven't had time since my kids were born." The assumption here is that politics is something you do for The World rather than for you and yours. Increasingly, however, I realize that parenting *is* my politics. I find my allies are those people who make my life as a parent easier whether it's an arms control advocate or a good teacher or someone like Bill Cosby, who can produce that rarest of all experiences, real family entertainment.

I respect people in public life who take care of their families as well as do their job. In this regard, I thought the much maligned Jackie Kennedy Onassis managed to maintain a strong family life against all odds. By contrast, I've been appalled at how few have observed the hypocrisy of Ronald Reagan advocating "family values" while seeming to be quite distant and unavailable to his own children. If someone spends his life making speeches and going to meetings while his own family is in shambles, I find it hard to take him seriously, like the preacher who can't practice what he preaches. It's clear to me that regardless of whatever happens in my life, I won't enjoy it unless my children are doing well.

At the end of the Bananas conference, many spoke of how comforting it was to spend time with other struggling parents, to understand how common the problems are. One father went up to one of the conference organizers and said, "I want you to know how much we appreciate what you're doing for people like us." Although working parents don't have much time for organizing and meeting, I think we are going to increasingly see the end of the parent as wimp. But first we're going to have to learn to stand up to our kids and set those limits. If they want to question authority, they can wait until they're capable of cleaning their rooms or proving themselves otherwise responsible. Once we earn a little self-respect at home, maybe then we can find a way to make our schools, our communities, and our governments help our lives as parents instead of make them more difficult.

Having a child helps you get your priorities straight. You know that you'll never waste a prayer on anything frivolous again. No more, please-God-let-me-get-the-promotion. Never another please-let-him-call-me. Anybody who's ever sat in a hospital emergency room waiting for the results of tests on their child knows exactly what I'm talking about. Although it's easy to forget, there is nothing more important we have to do than raise these children.

When I first walked around with my baby strapped on my chest in her little frontpack, I noticed a lot of people giving me a big smile. I'm not talking about the baby-worshipers who kitchy-cooed my little doll. I mean the other parents who gave me that knowing welcome-to-the-club look. We *are* in this together. We're making the same statement against the dark, violent world that seems to have forgotten the value of life.

All the Way Home

It was my maiden voyage, so to speak, my first time out. I was a literary virgin on my first book tour. My publisher was offering more than the opportunity to plug my book. What I had was a chance to see America quickly and concisely, like a lyric poem—four cities in five days, from the mountains to the prairies. Slam, bam, and, thank you, Uncle Sam.

The trip did involve risking my life on airplanes and, what seems to be an additional risk these days, risking my life at airports. But I was actually on an airplane alone, my first flight in eleven years sans children. Boy, was it easy. I just sat there and did what *I* wanted. Now I understood what the '80s were all about.

Exercising my newfound freedom, I opted not to watch the movie of the game of Clue. Instead, I read Garrison Keillor's *Happy to Be Here* (which I was). In addition to Boston, New York, and Chicago, I was going to Minnesota, my first time there. Yet another notch on my geographic gun.

Since it was spring, I also faced a Californian's worst fear: exposure to real winter. This would not be the play winter of the Sierras in the snow but the slushy gray urban winter in which one must actually function. I sat in the San Francisco airport counting how many years had gone by since I saw snow in its unnatural habitat. A decade. Could I still survive the frozen tundra of a Boston or Chicago spring?

On the airplane, as soon as I stopped composing mental haikus on the nature of the clouds as seen from close up, I got out the notebook I had purchased for my journal. I had not kept a journal since the day we moved from the bad neighborhood to the good in Chicago when I was thirteen. The night before the move I decided to burn my diaries—four years of seething pubescent angst up in smoke.

I set the blaze in my wastebasket. This was during my Sara Teasdale–Edna St. Vincent Millay phase and I was probably saying things in my head like: Ah, ashes, ashes be my lot / Since he shan't come back to Camelot. The diaries, however, contained such songs of innocence as: Vince Tumbarelli put his arm around me—am I still a virgin?

Shortly after igniting the pages of my young life, I heard my mother approach. Thinking I would douse the flame, I grabbed the large bottle of Shalimar cologne that sat on my dresser. Because I was not much of a chemist, I miscalculated the effect of cologne on fire. My mother opened the door as a raging inferno, a flame from floor to ceiling (albeit contained in the wastebasket), shot up in my room. I'll never forget the way she looked, her hair in large brush rollers, screaming hysterically from the other side of the flame.

I'm not sure if it was this little melodrama that led to a quarter-century hiatus in diary writing, but I was determined that my trip would alter that history. Besides, since becoming *A Writer* I had virtually stopped writing for fun (not to mention reading for no purpose). As I faced that first blank page I realized what an inhibition it was to the diarist to think that she might someday publish these intimate scribbles. Mentally, I composed the first sentence: I solemnly vow that what I write here is not for publication. But before I could even write the words, I began to imagine how they would look in print as the lead to the story about my first book tour.

I ditched the notebook and read a story in *U.S. News & World Report* about the underclass, the cycle of hopelessness that enchains inner-city blacks. Since I had no intention of writing a story on that subject, it was the closest to "fun" reading I had done in a long time. The charts and the statistics seemed to take some of the pain out of the devastating facts presented. This was a sad story but not about "us."

My friend Nina met me at the airport in Boston. After fifteen years in California she'd moved back East last fall, back home, in part to insure her kids get a good education. One look at Boston and it was obvious she was in the right neck of the woods. Half the *Boston Globe* seemed to be devoted to education stories. Most of the people on the street looked like geniuses or at least serious students of genius. That is, they were male and tweedy and had Harvard tattooed on their foreheads. But more surprising was how beautiful Boston looked with all the architectural restoration and improvement. The scale and elegance of the Back Bay houses recalled the mansard-roofed mansions along the Seine. Yuppies are no dummies. No wonder they all want to live here.

My hotel, the Lenox, right downtown, was perfect—just reeking of early Americana and Ye Olde This and That—Bostonian kitsch. Nina and I avoided the suggested cafés where we could get sprouts on pita and avocado, walnut, and chicken salad (I did not come from California to see a California satire) and stumbled upon some old, woody clamhouse with anchors, lanterns, and even an angel-headed bow (seaport satire). The chowder was astounding. The shrimp were even better. We kept ordering more plates and more fish and everything was terrific. The waitress, who must have had an IQ of 180, managed to hold down the packed room alone without missing an order even though we kept on asking for just one more thing. When we stepped out it was 1:00 A.M. and the last snow of the year was falling. I tasted snowflakes, the perfect dessert.

In the morning, after breakfast in the hotel dining room with twenty men all reading *The Wall Street Journal* (I read it, too, but skipped the numbers), I began my first day of radio and TV interviews. I took a stroll down that fine line between selling and selling out. That is, how much of an ass does one make of oneself in public to get a little attention and make a few bucks?

On a TV show, I followed a sixty-year-old Bulgarian woman who is an expert on the disease lupus erythematosus. I relaxed as I watched her contorted face on the monitor and appreciated how easy it would be to appear bright and sparkling. She was not, as they say, a tough act to follow.

In fact, I generally relaxed on the tour as I realized that many of the interviewers were only good little media Germans, just doing their job. It's not their job to be interesting. It's their job to fill up space. This was especially true of the TV people, who were, in some cases, terrified that *something* might happen. Content was not their bag. It should be noted, of course, that I was on the bozo circuit. I am not Gore Vidal and these people were not David Letterman or Oprah Winfrey.

Most of the interviewers had to struggle to categorize me. I had some sympathy with my hosts on this one since I have been working on that little problem for most of my life. I guess I most nearly fit the title "female humorist," which meant I was invariably described as a hip Erma Bombeck or a radical Erma Bombeck or a premenopausal Erma Bombeck. I consoled myself by thinking that they probably call Alice Walker the black Erma Bombeck and Anne Tyler the serious Erma Bombeck and Joan Didion the snotty Erma Bombeck and Philip Roth the masculine Erma Bombeck. And what of the real Erma? The Erma Bombeck Erma Bombeck.

Both the peak and the nadir of the tour came during my twenty-four-hour whirlwind through Minneapolis. My first sighting in the center of town was of a huge neon sign that said WONDER BREAD and the experience left me more firmly committed to You Are What You Eat than ever before.

Minneapolis is a great radio town and it was there I met a man who may be the most charming and amusing radio host in America. Roger Erickson, the morning commute voice of WCCO, is a classic midwestern dry wit. I was in his studio the morning the Marcoses' inventory was revealed and I will never forget Erickson's perfect radio voice announcing: "Five hundred black bras. Five hundred. Black ones." Our interview was interrupted by the farm reports and I got to banter with the reporter. "What exactly do you mean by the Daily National Slaughter?" I inquired. "Are we talking freeways, bars, or what?"

After all this good fun I was brought down to earth by the producer of a TV show called *Good Company*. The woman accosted me soon after I arrived at the studio. I should have known something was up when she told me to enter through the sliding glass doors at the rear of the studio. She had the worst case of humorophobia I've ever seen. Noting that the word *sarcasm* appeared in the title of my book, she asked point blank if I intended to actually *be* sarcastic. Because if I did, that wouldn't work. "I'll be honest," she said, "I have a space to fill." She wanted me to talk about parenting, a serious yet fun subject. "Be kinda light, kinda fun, but not sarcastic."

Soon I heard the announcer saying, "Next up is Alice Kahn, author of *Multiple* Scar*casm*—Scar*casm*—Scar—oh, well, Alice is going to talk about parental burnout." An instant expert on burnout, I entered a canvas tentlike structure where an allegedly live audience of the whitest people on earth sat in bleacher seats for this daytime TV circus.

I spoke sincerely about my life as a parent. "My kids say the darnedest things too." I answered questions from the audience. "What do you do when your kids are driving you crazy?" "Lock yourself in the bathroom and pray you don't harm them." How's that for sincerity?

I was followed by the spring fashion preview ("Socks are very big"), and was preceded by Jerry Jeff Walker, the folksinger, who was to sing his famous ballad about Mr. Bojangles Robinson. The same obnoxious producer rushed up to him before he even had time to remove his sunglasses. "Keep it down to two minutes," she told him.

"Whadaya mean?" he asked.

"Keep your song down to two minutes. Our musical segments are two minutes."

"But I can't do that," pleaded the artist.

"Skip the part where he dies," I advised.

Walker's escort from the Carleton, the nightclub where he was appearing, agreed to send me a T-shirt from the club with its motto "A touch of Vegas in Minnesota." The shirt now turns heads in San Francisco.

Back at my hotel, I read the tourist brochure, hoping to find a good spot for one of those famous egg salad sandwiches. But all the official guide would direct me to were "unique boutiques." Having just come through Boston and New York, I began to wonder just how many unique boutiques this country can hold before it sinks beneath an overload of costume jewelry and ceramic mugs.

I hit the streets and finally stopped at Mrs. Scandia's Smorgasbord, where the tuna salad was incomparable. While there I saw a family with two little girls the ages of my own daughters. It was the first time I realized how much I missed my family and I purchased a card with an outstanding example of Scandinavian troll art (a hot genre in these parts) to send them. It showed Mom and Pop Troll and the two little Troll girls picnicking on the edge of a cliff.

My last stop was Chicago, a place filled with emotion for me since I spent the first seventeen years of my life there and still tend to think of it as the scene of the crime. Like New York, Chicago seemed to be booming. (For more on New York, see F. A. Sinatra, "New York, New York.") The Gold Coast of Chicago looked more beautiful than ever. Boul Mich was also très yup. Bigger buildings. Grander stores. Neiman-Marcus next to Marshall Field across from Bonwit Teller. More places now serving

"California cuisine" and blackened redfish and angel hair pasta.
Store windows that exclaimed: Baguettes now!

One morning in Chicago, after doing a TV show in the suburbs and before taping a radio interview with a man who, despite
his trained voice and Waspish name I recognized as none other
than Nuggie Horowitz from my childhood, I took a detour from
my itinerary. I have to admit my view of America on this tour, a
view from good hotels and booming city centers, was softening
me on Reaganomics. To read about the record low unemploy-
ment rates in Boston, to see the massive downtown construction
in Minneapolis, to observe the Park Avenueing of lower Manhattan, the artistic renaissance in Chicago, you had to feel this country was on a roll. I asked my driver to leave the freeway so I could
see the house where I was born.

The neighborhood, a slum when I left it, was more depressed
than ever. In ghetto time, two generations of women who mother
young and men who die young had passed. Scores of men stood
around the streets and in the many vacant lots. Here there were
miles and miles of people shut out from that booming economy.
A banner hung from a building: PARK ROW—TRANSIENTS WELCOME
—18$ A NIGHT. Park Row had not gone condo.

The house, a ten-flat building, had been my father's pride. A
palace, he called it, a palace. "Take me to one, two, three, oh,
South Independence Boulevard," he would tell the cabdrivers.
"That's Moe Rosenberg's, the ward committeeman's, building."

I never thought our flat was a palace, but I liked the neighborhood where I grew up. I lived on the block. The center of my life
was my school where I learned I could be whatever I wanted. But
in the late '50s the neighborhood changed and almost overnight it
became a poor black slum. As part of the last white family on the
block, I was anxious for us to move away. Not that I felt threat-
ened, the ghetto wasn't terribly violent then. I just didn't like
being different.

I'd been back to the place twice since we moved. Once was in
the late '60s, after my father died and the riots had happened.

Most of the stores were gone, buildings were burned out or boarded up, and as I briefly paused in front of the house, a menacing group of teenagers wielding baseball bats approached me. I'd seen the words *Vicelord City* sprayed on the corner and beat it. Another time, in 1978, on a snowy day after my mother's funeral, we stopped and paid homage to the old house in what seemed to be an ever-worsening slum.

Twice, before I rushed on to my next interview, I asked the driver to circle the block looking for my house. The third time around, I accepted the truth. The building was gone. Ten apartments, now a mudhole. My old block was the worst-looking place in America I'd ever seen.

I don't know why it should hurt so. What did I expect—that we'd all move back some day? That we'd all live in peace, in harmony, the upwardly mobile generation who left and the hopelessly stagnant underclass now entrenched here?

The book tour was fun, a kind of triumphal march for a girl from a bad neighborhood. But of all that happened, all that made me feel love for this country—the wit of radio people, the acumen of taxi drivers who can reduce a town to a succinct summary of its scandals, the skill of waitresses who can balance a tray and a roomful of people, the conversations and accents of cities—of all that I saw in a blitz of images, that mudhole will be a thorn in my heart forever. If I hadn't lived there once, I might never have known. Because you can travel from town to town, from the mountains to the prairies, and never realize that the true democracy we sang about in grammar school pageants just isn't working.

III

---

*Everything You Ever
Wanted to Know
About Everything*

How to Raise
a Perfect CHUMP

Once life was simple, a man had a career and a woman had children. They fell in love, got married, had kids. (Okay, there are variations. People fell in love, *had* to get married, had kids.) Today we have more choices. A typical pattern—insofar as one can be said to exist—might look like this: Fall in love, fear commitment, break up, finish junior high, fall in love, break up, get B.A. in humanities, fall in love, explore bisexuality, break up, go to professional school, settle for best available partner, enjoy two-career-couple/big-pile-of-disposable-income *life-style*, go to should-I-have-a-baby therapy, plan birthing, have the kid, try to do children right, go nuts.

And that's just the man's pattern.

So what do you get when you rub two yuppies together? You get the perfect CHUMP—CHildren of Upwardly Mobile Professionals.

They've been called gourmet babies, children without childhood, and designer kids, but in many ways the CHUMP is just the spoiled brat with a slight variation. They may be living in a material world, but it is also a world filled with complex social relationships (divorce, lovers, au pair girls), terrifying urban characters (child molesters, night stalkers, homeless schizophrenics), and busy parents struggling to define New Parenting. No wonder these kids are ready for stress reduction by kindergarten.

It's a Tina Turner kind of world our thoroughly modern little Sarahs and Seans are living in—nobody does anything nice and easy anymore. Every moment of Today's Child Raising is fraught with choices—make a wrong choice, the kid goes to hell in a hand basket. (Make that a handwoven wicker bassinet, $139.95, available from *The Whole Perfect Child Catalog.*) A look at the incredible selection of parenting books gives you an idea of how complicated things have gotten. The fact that there's a book called *How to Get Pregnant* tells you how far from the level of instinct we have progressed.

Assuming one is clever enough to figure out how egg and sperm arrange a meeting, you move on to titles like *Nourishing Your Unborn Child.* Drinking milk and eating vegetables are no longer enough. The pregnant mother is now thinking for two. It's not IQ that will determine whether the fetus will go to Harvard—it's what the mother reads. A Jackie Collins reader has probably sentenced her unborn child to the cultural cesspool.

If you haven't totally messed things up before your child is born, you're ready to move into books like *Pregnancy as Healing and Birthing Normally.* (When will someone write a book called *The Gerunding of Childhood?*) The astonishing number of books telling people how to get the kid out contribute to the widespread belief that birthing is the main event. They distract people from the twenty or so years of indentured servitude that begin immediately after labor and delivery.

All this fuss about natural childbirth and nontraumatic delivery is a direct result of sexual liberation. Once women started demanding foreplay, an Alternative Birthing Center was virtually a fait accompli. If the woman was going to be involved in sex, then gosh darn it, the man better well be involved in birth.

I myself was probably the last woman on earth to have a baby the old-fashioned way. As I was wheeled into the delivery room eleven years ago, the delivery room head nurse (a large, frightening Dickensian character who went by the name of "Mother") began to push me down and apply restraints to my hands and legs. I was accompanied by both my husband and my friend Phyllis, a Ph.D. in maternity nursing. Phyllis was there ostensibly as my "labor coach" but really to protect my ass and teach the hospital staff new childbirth methods. As my husband began doing his Lamaze breathing (to keep from fainting), Phyllis went up to the crusty old nurse and said, "Recent studies indicate that allowing the mother to sit up enables gravity to aid the birthing process." The nurse hesitated, then turned to her assistant and sneered, "Strap her down."

I probably could have used books like *Silent Nights for You and Your Baby*, *Improving Your Child's Behavior Chemistry*, *Toilet Learning*, *Playful Parenting*, *How to Raise a Responsible Child*, *Cry Babies*, *Bringing Up a Moral Child*, and *Helping Your Child Grow Slim*. And reading *Circumcision: The Painful Dilemma*—so what if I had a girl; it never hurts to be informed—would also have been useful. But none of these books was available a decade ago. I was ahead of the baby boomlet, walking alone through the minefield of parental choices.

Look at the breast versus bottle controversy. Oddly enough, at the same time that women became working mothers, there was a sharp rise in social taboos against convenience products in child raising. Taking out an artificial bottle containing artificial formula in the '80s is as shocking a sign of Bad Womaning as going topless was in the '50s. The mother who bottle-feeds her baby these days had better be prepared for the guilt that comes when a friend brags, "I nursed my baby until he was forty-seven."

In the past decade, the baby-products market has become a $14 billion industry. And once your child is old enough to think for herself or himself (or to watch television) the manufacturers will drop you like yesterday's diaper and begin to appeal directly to the child, that veritable Frankenstein monster of a consumer you have created. How many of us, who postponed childbirth for years, only to have one or two perfect children, can be so abusive as to deny the little darlings anything?

If you are a professional, you have probably learned to divide all people into two groups: those whom you want something from and those who want something from you. Children are definitely in the latter group. In fact, they want it all—your love, your attention, and your money. Estimates on how much they want (sometimes called the Cost of Raising a Child) range from $20,000 to $250,000. (And that's not counting styling mousse or earrings.) So while other experts will help you raise a moral child or a gifted child or an obedient child, let me point out the essentials of an upscale child:

The Importance of Wearing Oshkosh B'Gosh. The CHUMP must be instilled from the earliest months with the necessity of wearing what's "in." It needn't be practical, just trendy—like those Swatch watches nobody can read. It needn't be expensive, but the label must be prominently displayed on the outside of the garment. This is confusing for people who grew up in the era when labels were sewed inside. Oshkosh B'Gosh overalls are absolutely de rigueur once the child is out of Carters but too small for Guess or Esprit. A few little shares in Oshkosh B'Gosh tucked in the bib pocket wouldn't be a bad idea either. The stock's gained five points since going public a few months ago. That's big bucks, b'gosh!

The Right Stuffing. The child who is ignorant of good taste in food is ignorant of all good taste and therefore deserves to spend the rest of his life in the Barbie-and-Ken hellhole of fast franchised foods. Can your baby say: "K-Paul," "bar and grill," "caffè latte," "albacore with salsa fresca," "cilantro garnish," "blackened redfish," "bottled water"?

If so, he is ready to pass the sushi test. First, you make him eat it; then you tell him what it is. If he says "yuck," he is an ordinary child and must be gradually introduced to nouvelle baby cuisine. Start with pureed kiwi then proceed to mashed quail.

*_The Designing Kid._ A sense of form without content is necessary to appreciate the beauty in urban life. Explain to your child that the city isn't a concrete jungle of buildings, but rather that it is filled with Architecture. Get your child's colors done. Cultivate an appreciation of trends in design. An outstanding example: My little friend Lily, who is four, picked up an Elmore Leonard paperback and commented on the murder scene on the cover. "_Miami Vice_ art," she said.

*_Remembrance of Things Past._ Nostalgia for the golden ages he didn't experience is essential to the CHUMP's sophisticated posture of terminal insouciance. The CHUMP must learn to regard the '50s as a pastel-colored paradise populated by happy people like Marilyn Monroe and James Dean. The '60s, he must learn, was a funny time when hippies in unpegged pants talked about silly things like peace.

*_Outdoorsy Is Funsy._ Valuable time is wasted in the first nine months of life being sedentary. Your child should learn to kayak before he can walk. Or put him in a bobsled and just let him go. Toss him in the pool and see where instinct leads him. This will teach the CHUMP to be tough. Someday he'll make a great macho yuppie. That's someone who walks into a bar and says, "I'll have a chenin blanc—and make it a double."

*_Exposure to Privates._ There's no point in sending CHUMPs to public schools. Public schools are for poor people and guilty liberals. They won't help the kid get into Princeton.

Finally, I'd be remiss if I concluded without emphasizing that you should always present your child a list of choices. Never decide for him and never—under any circumstances—use the word _no_ in your child's presence. The child who learns the meaning of the word _no_ might get the bizarre impression that the world is not his oyster bar. After all, it takes a chump to make a CHUMP.

The End Is Near

Jesus had them and so did Moses. Marilyn Monroe, Albert Einstein, Karl Marx, and Joan of Arc had them. Ronald Reagan is still having them and, presumably, so is his wife, Nancy. But dare we speak of them except in jokes and whispers? We can talk about child molesters, nuclear megatonnage, and even sadomasochism more easily than we can talk about bowel movements—the last frontier.

To give you an idea of how serious the situation is, consider this: Yesterday I turned to my husband and said, "Hey, honey, how about a nice tasteful article about bowel movements?" He: "Sure, if you want to ruin your career." And even you are perhaps thinking: Oh, no—bowel movements! She's gone too far this time. But "too far" is where we want to go; so, reminding you that while you are what you eat, you aren't what you write about, let's get on with it: bowel movements, the unspeakable truth about real life.

First let me parade my expert credentials. I am, in real life, a registered nurse, which makes me in the popular mind a virtual Ph.D. in Movement Studies. Ah, now you get it! Now you are having visions of me in knee-length white polyester running after you deadpan with a bedpan. This, of course, is the cartoon image of my profession, but as a result of it I have been privy, so to speak, to our culture's deepest repression.

There is nothing people want to talk to nurses about more than their bowel movements. And what an untapped depth of descriptive power and metaphorical vision the average person can call forth on this subject. You simply would not believe it. I recall reading that Coleridge kept elaborate diaries of his and apparently renewed the old poetic license in these colorful exercises. Literary scholars tell me that these journals make the "damsel with a dulcimer" stuff read like cold potatoes. As a health-care professional, I can assure you that when it comes to describing bowel movements even the most ordinary slob has Coleridge potential.

Rather than continue to discuss this terribly important subject in a first-person manner—after all who wants to read another My Greatest or The Most Unforgettable story?—let's look at the health implications. The National Commission on Digestive Diseases reported to Congress in 1979 that there were an estimated 34 million people diagnosed as having gastrointestinal-tract diseases. Although these diseases are now considered common, they were unusual or nonexistent before this century. A leading expert in this area, Dr. Denis Burkitt, places the blame for this epidemic on our refined-products/low-fiber diet and the resulting problem of constipation. Put another way: Where have all the croissants gone?

Now this Dr. Burkitt, a surgeon and epidemiologist, is one dedicated scientist. To prove his theories he went around the world weighing the stools of various peoples and correlating that data with information about their diet. When he got to Africa he found almost no disease in the digestive tract and the biggest, bulkiest, greatest stools on earth. Consequently Burkitt has made it his life work to promote a high-fiber diet to Westerners.

Other researchers are now straining to prove that Burkitt's

findings have particular relevance for the most common digestive disease—some would say the most common disease in Western culture—hemorrhoids. And why am I laying this bummer on you? Because you, my fellow baguette-biting, over-thirty stool-strainers are entering the peak risk years. It's only a matter of time before you will be introduced as "Dirk Miller, Stanford M.B.A., telecommunications expert, software consultant, and hemorrhoid sufferer." The medical textbook *Diseases of the Colon and Anorectum* states that "Most people develop hemorrhoids of some degree beginning about age twenty, which become progressively larger during their physically active life." Robert Holt in his non-bestselling book *Hemorrhoids: A Cure and Preventative* reports: "In reviewing the records of patients with hemorrhoids, it was found that 80 percent of the patients were between the ages of thirty and sixty." And finally, this bomb from a leading proctologist in Grand Rapids: "One hundred percent of the population has hemorrhoids."

Unlike other digestive diseases, hemorrhoids were not unknown in the past. While no pharaohs have been found with a supply of Preparation H for the next world, the Bible contains this early description of the Lord's fury: ". . . he [God] smote the men of the city both small and great, and they had hemorrhoids in their secret parts . . . and the cry of the city went up to heaven" (I Samuel 5:9,12). Now, no amount of Metamucil can bail you out of that. Medical historian Rudolph Marx provides us with a whole new perspective on Waterloo: "Napoleon's painful piles, which he had had since his youth, were so inflamed from the opium given him to relieve his suffering, that he couldn't get out of bed, let alone sit on his horse." And those of us with brain cells enough left to remember the Carter administration have theorized that it was ultimately a hemorrhoid that brought Ronald Reagan into office.

But while hemorrhoids, commonly called "piles," have a long and glamorous history, the incidence of hemorrhoids (how widespread are they?) remains confused. This discrepancy—some claim an epidemic, others go so far as to call them "normal"—is due to a disagreement on the very basic question: What is a hemorrhoid? You'd think somebody would have had time between the Old Testament and now to figure out that one, but it turns out we hardly know our anus from our elbow! Really. And now we come to the heavy investigative part of my story.

Until the last year or so, virtually everyone who was anyone in proctology described hemorrhoids as swollen veins in the rectum, comparable to varicose veins in the leg. But leave it to our allies in England to get to the bottom of this. "Wrong!" cry the Brits to the varicose vein theory. "Bloody wrong." Here we see how the code of silence has inhibited our understanding and possibly contributed to the $80 million per year Americans spend on unproven hemorrhoid cures from laxatives to Preparation H. In searching the medical literature, I was unable to find a major review article on hemorrhoids written in the last few years in this country, and found only four pieces in the popular press in the last decade.

On the other hand, the British journal *The Practitioner* contained a revolutionary article, "Haemorrhoids and All That," in which a Dr. Thomson described hemorrhoids as a disturbance in "a structure yet to find its proper place in the anatomical lexicon —the anal cushion." His associate Dr. Alexander-Williams goes even further when he suggests in an article, "The Nature of Piles," in a prestigious British medical journal, that rather than a disease what we have here are anatomical variations of what is normal. Alexander-Williams writes, in that engaging manner even doctors master in England, "Few who reach middle age can claim never to have had any symptoms related to the anus. Thomson has shown elegantly, if not originally, that what many regard as piles are normal vascular cushions. We all have them, and they are as natural as the vascular cushions at the upper end of the alimentary tract we call lips. We are prepared to accept a wide variety of lips: thin lips, pouting lips, petulant lips, wet lips, and even hot lips. Similarly, variations in the vascular cushions at the anus should possibly be regarded as signs of character rather than disease."

While this new insight may explain the inflated estimates on the incidence of hemorrhoids, it is of little comfort to those with a pain in the cushion. The pain occurs when something disturbs the tone of the anal sphincter enough to cause displacement, enlargement, and even thrombosis of one of several anal cushions. Hard bowel movements remain the leading candidate for this no-whoopee-cushion situation. In addition to severe pain, other symptoms associated with hemorrhoids include the alarming one of rectal bleeding and the socially disruptive problem of rectal itching.

Unfortunately these British doctors, so skillful at looking into the rectum and describing areas previously uncharted through centuries of suffering, offer no significant insights into prevention and treatment of the symptoms associated with disturbances in the anal cushions. One could get about as much help from a salesman at Pillow Park as from Alexander-Williams's observation on the etiology of hemorrhoids: "I suspect that emotional tension plays a part, and I have a syndrome that I designate with the eponym YETAS, the young executive tight-anus syndrome. Certainly this seems to be one group of people prone to piles; others are golfers and professional cricketers." So now you know: You plays your cricket, you takes your chances.

For that great suffering mass of nonexecutive, noncricketing people, we must return to the work of Burkitt for advice on how to prevent this common, painful, but not life-threatening disorder. *Health Facts*, a consumer-oriented bulletin, notes: "Within the last decade, the medical profession has made a complete reversal of its standard dietary recommendations to those with digestive diseases and disorders. For years physicians' advice to people with anything from ulcers to diverticulosis was to consume a refined, soft diet. There is now mounting evidence that this type of diet may actually be the *cause* of most, if not all, digestive diseases. The high-fiber diet, i.e. predominantly whole grains, fresh vegetables, and fruit, has been identified as the best preventive measure against most intestinal disorders." While constipation, defined as hard stools (not necessarily infrequent stools), is what's knocking our anal cushions out of place, who among us is prepared to abandon our refined-products diet that leads to this "garbage-in/nothing-out" syndrome?

Many of us gave up white flour once already. There was a trend not too long ago to regard white processed grain as something only ignorant, manipulated people ate. This was replaced by the incredible boom in French-style bread and rolls like croissants and brioches. Delicious, yes, but no more healthy than Wonder Bread. But one can hardly suggest not eating these things without appearing to be some overbearing *nurse* or something. I mean, it's okay to tell people not to smoke, but can you imagine a sign in a fashionable restaurant saying "Thank you for not eating refined white flour products"?

We are going to have to look at the relationship between intake and output either before or after we get hemorrhoids because the treatments, even the latest treatments, just aren't a lot of laughs. Improved surgical techniques such as cryosurgery—using liquid nitrogen to freeze the lesion—or "rubber band litigation" are still not painless. Many doctors believe it's pointless to use surgery if the underlying dietary problems are not corrected. Instead, they use a variety of salves, sitz baths (a bath as hot as you can sitz in), and stool softeners as palliative treatments. I just received an ad for a new product that touts itself as an alternative to the "400,000 hemorrhoidectomies performed in the US annually." The product, Cold Stick, is a kind of reusable frozen finger of ice. Any way you look at it, the treatment issue is not a pretty picture.

For those of you who have stuck with me in this groundbreaking discussion, the end is near. If God smote us with those hemorrhoids, we're not likely to see them disappear overnight. But I do know this: Until we can speak about bowel movements with people other than nurses, the problem will remain on the back burner. That's why I want everyone reading this to consider him- or her- (or whatever) self to be the vanguard of Bowel Movement Liberation. And, I want all you libbers, those of you who know in your hearts that what goes in must come out, to turn to your neighbor, wherever you are, and shake that neighbor's hand and say, "Let's talk about bowel movements now."

Day Care Nightmares

While skin cancer seems to have replaced terrorism and child molestation as the media's favorite nightmare, not too long ago you couldn't read a paper or watch TV news without concluding that the bogeyman lives. Daily stories of adults who molest, rape, imprison, sodomize, and beat innocent children trigger an almost visceral desire for justice. Especially alarming have been the much publicized cases that remind us that, among its myriad forms, the bogeyman may be a lady operating a child-care facility.

For working parents, these stories are particularly horrifying. Child care is the lifeblood of the working parent, a necessary component of the family's psychological well-being. And for many working families, child care is also essential to their economic survival. While some parents have managed to combine work and family by working at home or leaving the children with a grandparent, these are the exceptions. The vast majority rely on some form of paid child care—frequently from strangers. In this context, the media focus on child abuse and molestation takes on a new and ominous meaning. As parents are bombarded with front-page stories presenting the sordid details of grotesque child abuse cases, they must also ask themselves: In seeking child care, am I risking *this?*

It was after I had tormented myself for weeks by following the details of the case of Tara Burke, a preschooler who was kidnapped and molested, that I began to realize that reading these stories was affecting me in a way similar to the way I suspect the media coverage of AIDS has affected many homosexuals. What I learned about Tara Burke was that just over the hill from my home, in a suburban shopping center, a child the same age as mine had been snatched from her parents' car and held prisoner in a filthy van for almost a year. At two and a half she was forced to perform sexual acts and was beaten when she refused. When the men accused of doing this to her, Alex Cabarga and "Treefrog" Johnson, were arrested, I found myself waking up at night having fantasies of vengeance. I would picture myself as part of a mob stoning them to death.

When the Lori Nathan case broke last year, I decided I'd finally had enough. Once I realized the salient facts—that for years this woman had operated a day-care home where she routinely beat children—that was it. Every time I saw Lori Nathan's name in the newspaper I quickly turned the page. If I saw her on TV, I jumped up and changed the channel. Then a few months ago, sordid allegations began to surface about what went on at a licensed day-care facility in Los Angeles run by a seventy-six-year-old grandmother named Virginia McMartin. "Authorities charged that for at least a decade more than 100 children were fondled, sodomized, raped, and there are suspicions that some of the tots may have been hired out for pornography and prostitution," *Newsweek* reported. That was it; time to stop reading and switch off the set.

And perhaps this was more media sensationalism than fact. Subsequent to the *Newsweek* article, the charges against McMartin and all but two of her colleagues were dropped.

"The Far Right is loving this. It's like a fundamental evangelist saying, 'See, you sinners—you leave your children and this is what you get.' " The speaker was June Sale, director of UCLA Child Care Services. Sale quickly added, "The fact is that most children are molested at home by a relative or friend, not in an institutional setting." Nonetheless, child-care workers are reporting a sharp increase in parental anxiety and suspicion that they feel is potentially harmful to everyone involved, particularly the children.

June Sale was one of a small group of child-care specialists who met informally recently for a daylong discussion of what they termed "child abuse hysteria." Arlyce Currie, one of the directors at Bananas, an innovative child-care services agency that called the meeting, told me, "We did it because of the growing climate of distrust among parents and child-care providers. I'm getting a record number of calls from parents who are using child care for the first time, asking me, 'How do I know they aren't child abusers? How will I *really* know?' There is a new, higher level of fear than we have ever seen before."

Currie objects to what she feels is a misplaced focus in response to the media blitz of stories about child sexual abuse cases and the nightmarish reports about child-care centers. "There has been a narrow, vigilante response—all the focus is on reporting, on placing responsibility for it on the child," said Currie.

Attempts to encourage children to tell do, of course, seem worthwhile if the results are the prosecution and conviction of abusers. However, as public policy analyst David Kirp commented in the Sacramento *Bee*, this is not always the case:

"When a report is filed," Kirp wrote, "a train of investigation is set in motion. Friends, neighbors, teachers, doctors get quizzed. That has to be traumatic for those caught up in the process. And things become worse for the 400,000 American families compelled to accept treatment under the threat of court action; a study conducted for the National Center on Child Abuse and Neglect found that in about half of these cases, the children had never been maltreated. . . .

"If the rules now on the books really protected children in

danger, some of this overprotection might be tolerable. They don't, though, for the minor complaints swamp the system, leaving the real danger signals too often unspotted. Serious cases get lost in the shuffle."

Currie is also concerned about the effect of the child-abuse panic on workers in child-care centers. "I'm worried about the potential backlash against men, in general, and gay men in particular. We've tried so hard to make men feel comfortable performing nurturing roles. Now everyone is feeling skittish." June Sale says the men working at her center held a meeting and talked about their fears and vulnerability. "They decided that they wanted to have a woman present every time they provided personal care such as diapering a child." This situation, reminiscent of the male gynecologist's need for a woman in the room when he examines a patient's pelvis, represents a trend toward a more procedures-oriented, defensive approach to child care.

This clinical approach worries Marcy Whitebook, director of the Child Care Employee Project in Oakland. She described a social worker who told the employees of an infant center, "Don't touch, hold, or kiss the kids." Whitebook is also concerned about the demoralizing effect of child-abuse stories on workers in the field. "Child care is an undervalued form of work. It has been thought of as unskilled 'women's work.' The pay is not good, the status is not good. The only good thing about it is the chance to have a close relationship with kids. And now we're saying closeness with kids is dangerous." Whitebook quickly added, "Even as I say this I can hear a voice asking, 'What do you mean by *close* to kids?' If you say anything critical about how the situation is being dealt with, it's almost like you're coming out in favor of child abuse."

Those who attended the meeting are concerned that children are being taught to look upon all touching and affection with suspicion, that they are being encouraged to be defensive and on their guard at all times. "It's complicated," said Whitebook. "For example, we do want our children to know that if we are, say, tickling them, and they don't like it, then they have a right to say, 'Stop. That's it. No more.' On the other hand, if they need a diaper change, it's got to be done whether they like it or not."

The current emphasis on reporting alone, the child-care workers fear, will lead to more like accusations and destroyed lives without affecting the actual incidence of abuse. Once accused, few are ever really able to clear their names even if investigations prove them innocent.

Carol Casady, a family services worker in a remote California county, represented the concerns of rural areas at the meeting—concerns that turn out to be not so different from those of urban areas, except for the almost complete lack of treatment and support services in rural counties. She also expressed the concern that homosexual men—treated as suspect in the first place—would become targets in a witch-hunt atmosphere. She described a case where a male teacher was dismissed as a molester based on circumstantial reports from male students. "I think the students were out to get him for something."

"It's interesting," observed Marcy Whitebook, "but I suspect that people who are against sex education in the schools would welcome sexual assault training. I think they want people to feel badly about sexuality, but I can't prove that."

As the mother of a child who is just now finishing nursery school, I have been impressed with what an intense interest in sex there is at this age. Recently, when we were at the beach, my daughter put a bunch of sand in the crotch of her bathing suit and said laughingly, "This is my penis." While I hoped nobody near us heard that, I recognized it as the kind of game she'd probably been playing at her nursery school.

Although a rarity a generation ago, nursery and preschool is pretty much the rule for children today. Prior to nursery school, parents use a variety of child-care situations, from large centers to baby-sitters at home. Both my children had been in playgroups from the time they could walk. Playgroups are informal child-care groups in which each parent in the group cares for the children (usually three to five of them) in her home for a morning or longer. At about age two and a half to three (when they are generally out of diapers in the daytime) children begin nursery school.

My children went to the New School, a nearby nursery school, which in many ways is typical of small community child-care centers. Located in a little redwood building that it rents from a Unitarian church, the school and day-care center is surrounded by beautiful trees and flowering bushes. On one side of the building is a large grassy yard; on the other side the three schoolrooms open up onto another yard, part of which is concrete for riding tricycles, the rest sandy and filled with several large climbing structures created by carpenter parents. There is a small vegetable garden for the children to plant the seeds they sprout and an area full of rabbit cages. Every morning, children line up for a chance to feed and hold a bunny.

One of the schoolrooms has blocks, a costume trunk, a playhouse, and mats for tumbling. The other two classrooms are cluttered with tables, chairs, books, and toys; the walls are covered with kids' art—every piece of it beautiful and unique. The children divide up into "the big kids," the four-year-olds, and "the little kids," the three-year-olds. The New School is flexible enough to accommodate a wide range of parent needs. There is child care available from 7:30 A.M. for parents who must leave for work, a nursery school in the morning, and afternoon child care as needed up to 5:30 P.M. The school also picks up children from nearby elementary schools for afterschool care.

This particular school began as a parent cooperative in the early '70s, and although it has changed with the times, it still reflects the nonauthoritarian attitude of that era. There seem to be only three serious rules: keep the gate closed, don't hurt anyone, and never bring foods with sugar. After that, the main goal of the school is to help children have fun. There are organized activities such as book reading, music, art projects, trips to the Y for kindergym, the Lawrence Hall of Science for study projects (such as dinosaurs or space), the Pacific Film Archive for movies, or Tilden Park for nature walks. But the real learning is in how to get along with others.

Part of this socialization process requires dealing with the obvious curiosity children of this age have about each other's bodies. I have seen some of this come out in amusing ways, such as the "penis derision" my daughter displayed at the beach. There's also great curiosity about how the opposite sex uses the bathroom. Earlier this year some of us discussed our concern with the games of "doctor" we discovered the children were having behind the wooden playhouse. The director of the school proposed the children be allowed to continue, with two rules: Children should be encouraged to say no if they are feeling coerced, and an adult should be present. One teacher used the occasion to teach sophisticated anatomy lessons; I discovered this after my daughter announced to me proudly, "I can have babies because I have a uterus."

I visited the New School to interview one of the child-care workers, Ray Sundance, about the current abuse panic. I didn't know much about Sundance other than that he was a big, soft-looking man who often wore funny hats; that he had two sons and a famous father (journalist Dave Dellinger, one of the "Chicago Seven" from the Vietnam era); and that he had refused to accept his B.A. from Yale in 1969 as a war protester. Sundance has worked at the New School for six years, and during this time I have observed his firm but very affectionate approach, especially with some of the school's most difficult youngsters.

He told me he shared Marcy Whitebook's concerns about potential damage to children in the atmosphere of panic. "I think teaching the children to say no is the key to this thing. Teaching them that they don't have to keep it a secret if someone approaches them. But I think telling them no one is to see or touch your private parts is the wrong message. For example, there is a lot of good touching that takes place among the children themselves. There is also a need for parents to check their children for lice, for pinworms, for infections. And this means looking at their whole body. I think the idea that the private parts are special and should never be touched is the wrong message."

Sundance described a situation in which a child was yelling at another on the playground. "I walked up to Anna and touched her back to make contact. I began to rub it in what I thought was a friendly way. Then she said, 'I don't like it when men touch me that way.' To me, that was fine. 'Your body is yours' is the right message; but don't pick out the genitals. Don't go back to antisex messages."

Sundance acknowledged that he is aware of the possibility that his affection and touching of children might be misconstrued as molestation. However, he said he feels safer now than when he started working with children because there are more men in child care. He doesn't think he's been affected by the current wave of hysteria because "I've been here for a long time. People have had plenty of chances to observe me. If someone accused me of something, there are others who would back me up."

While we were sitting and talking in the block room at the nursery school, it was clear to me why I have never worried about my child's safety at this facility. June Sale and Arlyce Currie emphasize that the much publicized recent cases of child abuse took place at centers that limited parents' visiting hours, that had areas that were off limits to parents and were used by parents who didn't know each other and had little contact with each other. In contrast, my daughter's nursery school is minutes from my door. My older daughter went there and my friends' kids did too. Most of the children—and, more importantly, most of the workers—live in the neighborhood. For many families, the nursery school is a focus of social life with potlucks, bazaars, and weekend trips organized by the school community. It is a parent-participation school, and although I find it hard to be around the chaos and energy of that many preschoolers, I've always felt welcomed and encouraged to come. I have appreciated the loving attention my children have received there. Their teachers have seemed to say to me: I love your child and I can show it. No big deal.

I asked Ray Sundance why he thinks child abuse is receiving so much attention now. "The news media is so unimaginative," he said, "that if *Newsweek* does it, every paper does it. But it's a complicated message we're getting as child-care workers, and that may be correct—real messages *are* confusing. The message I get is, be nurturing but not sexually involved. Actually, I think the attention focused on child molestation is a good thing. Sexual abuse comes out of the historical acceptance that men are the possessors of women and children. So I'm glad to see this. It's an attack on the traditional patriarchal structure."

June Sale, on the other hand, fears the current atmosphere of suspicion "is a putdown on women *and* men. People are beginning to feel that if you care about children, if you want to be affectionate with them, there must be something wrong with you." She is also concerned that we are frightening very young children at the age when learning to trust is their major developmental task. "In their panic, parents are saying to children, 'If anyone touches you, I want you to tell me' or 'You might be kidnapped walking down the street without me.' At least when it happens on TV it isn't real. Now, we're saying it *is* real and you've got to defend yourself. Can we really expect that of a three-year-old?"

Like most of the others I spoke with, Sale emphasized that while the problem of child abuse is real and must be faced, she objects to the focus on reporting rather than prevention. "If parents had more support they'd be able to make better decisions. Let's provide that support. Let's bring in all the families at risk—and most working families are at risk, need help—let's bring them in and educate them as to their choices. Some parents are so desperate, they'll take anything. That's why we have so many latchkey kids. But we're not as interested in providing support and prevention as we are in reporting and punishing."

When Sale talked about desperation, it hit home. I thought

about the women I know who are in their late thirties, have jobs, and are pregnant for the first time. When I've asked these women what their plans are, the usual response is "When my six weeks' maternity leave is up, I'll put the baby in child care," as if "child care" is a magic solution that will just be there when they need it. The greatest fantasy many pregnant women have during that time when the imagination seems particularly ripe is that of a fairy godmother called child care—when, in fact, child-care solutions frequently are found only after an agonizing and guilt-ridden search.

With my first daughter, I was spoiled. I actually did find a fairy godmother—a woman I met in a playground with a baby the same age as mine. She was willing to care for my daughter while I went back to school. She charged only a small fee and mainly wanted a companion for her child. She clearly loved children. But with my second daughter I found no such baby-sitter *ex machina*. I had to search the big impersonal world for one. An ad in the paper caught my eye: "Registered nurse will care for your child in her home."

A nurse myself, I was a sucker for the RN credential—and I was desperate. My four-month maternity leave would be up in a few weeks; I had a part-time job to return to and no one to watch my baby. My husband could care for her in the evening when he returned from work, but due to a combination of exhaustion and breast-feeding I had not been away from her for more than a few hours. So, although I knew nothing about this person, I phoned her and arranged to bring my baby over for a trial.

As I approached her house I noticed that overflowing garbage cans had spilled out onto the path leading to her door. That made me uneasy, but I told myself I was just being uptight, an overprotective mother. *You've got to cut the cord*, I thought. When I met the woman, I had a bad feeling about her. Her apartment was cluttered and dirty. *Well, I'm not perfect myself*, I thought. Still, she seemed spacy and slow. Her professional nursing experience, she explained, had been with dying and unconscious patients. Now she cared for three infants and she showed me their cribs lined up in her dining room. One was crying loudly, another had a thick discharge from his nose. From the odor, the third needed a diaper change pronto. As we were talking a male friend of the woman dropped by to chat.

Although everything I saw made me feel uneasy, I'd spent the previous day fantasizing about what it would be like to be on my own again for two whole hours. I thought I'd jog for an hour and then leisurely read the newspaper and sip coffee somewhere with other grown-ups. I craved that little bit of carefree time and steeled myself to defend it. So instead of telling myself, *This feels wrong—look around some more*, I said to myself, *You've got to get away sometime.* I handed my baby, Hannah, to the woman.

I walked out the door and started jogging up to a track, about a mile and a half away. As I ran I tried to relax and enjoy the weightless feeling of not having a frontpack, a backpack, an umbrella stroller, or a baby in my arms for the first time in months. But instead of freedom I felt oddly empty.

I reviewed the complaints I'd tried to dismiss as trivial, as being too picky, as overprotective (that terrible thing only mothers are), as uptight. The place was dirty, the woman was spacy, she had too many infants—one of whom seemed quite sick—and she was entertaining a male guest. After fifteen minutes of jogging with this on my mind, I realized I not only had failed to achieve a runner's high but was fast approaching panic. I turned around and headed back to the woman's house, running faster than I ever had, singing a little nursery song I had made up for my daughter over and over in my mind. It was to the tune of Hari Krishna and it went *Hanny Bano, Hanny Bano, Bano Bano, Hanny Bano . . .*

When I got to the house, I pounded on the door, no longer caring if I appeared crazy or rude. I wanted to know my child was all right. I could hear babies crying inside. Was one of them mine?

It took an interminable time for the woman to answer. What was she doing in there? Was she trying to cover something up?

Finally, I was let in and grabbed Hannah and hugged her to me. I didn't have any real proof of any wrongdoing, but that's not the point. The point is that I had failed to trust my own instincts.

A few days later I called a friend, an intelligent woman I had known for years who had raised two children, and asked her if she would consider watching my child while I worked. I offered her a third of my salary, which seemed a pathetic wage for a woman of her capabilities but was still more than the going rate for child care. In the light of my frightening recent experience, I was suddenly struck by how little we value the people who care for our children. Why do we think child care should come dirt cheap?

I had also learned that there is no peace of mind when you doubt that your child is in good hands away from you. Although economic and other desperation may drive people to take chances, it's never worth it to leave your child in a situation that seems wrong.

Arlyce Currie said something that really spoke to my experience: "Parents are shaky about their instincts. They don't trust themselves, so they ask a friend who they think is a good mother what to do and then do what she does. But I don't think you can really rely on a friend's opinion if you don't check out the child-care situation yourself. One day care operator played off against the parents' mistrust of their own judgments. When parents would tell her that their child was crying and didn't want to come to child care, she'd turn it all back on them and say, 'He's fine when he's with me. Guess what he tells me about you?' "

"Even if we eventually develop a national child-care policy, we will still need to address the complex issue of children and sexuality—of when touching, cuddling, and kissing are appropriate," says Marcy Whitebook. With 1.3 million reported incidents of child abuse in 1983 alone, the problem seems unlikely to disappear. With a growing number of our infants and young children spending significant portions of their time in child care, can we find a solution that will insure that our children will get the loving care they need to thrive but will still be protected from abuse?

I don't have the answers to these questions, but I do know this: Children can suffer as much from no touching as they can from forced sexuality. When I was in nursing school, we did part of our pediatric training at a naval hospital. The most common diagnosis of the children admitted there was "failure to thrive," a condition of listlessness, poor growth, and immaturity that occurs in children who are neglected as well as in those who are abused. Many of these children had been left in their cribs all day with bottles propped up beside them.

I particularly remember one little girl, a beautiful child of about two. She never talked, but whenever anybody walked by her crib she would stand up and hold her arms outstretched, begging to be hugged. That was her treatment. We nursing students and the corpsmen who worked in the hospital spent as much time as we could holding and hugging her.

I think it's important to understand what the concerned child-care workers I interviewed were saying. I don't think anybody doubts the existence of child abuse and the need to find and punish abusers. But in our zealous and angry effort to solve the problem, let's not make all children victims.

Heavy Traffic
(School for Scoundrels)

I parked my car about a block from campus like any other school-girl, but I parked it very carefully. And even though it was five minutes to six, I put a nickel in the meter. I was going strictly by the book. I was turning a new leaf. You see, I wasn't just some reentry woman coming to Cal to brush up on Serbo-Croatian basketry. I was a Bad Girl on my way to reform school. In my heart I wore the big *V* for Violator. I was heading for the California Institute of Traffic Safety.

Trotting up Durant Avenue, grasping my notebook and swinging my backpack, I felt I blended in nicely with the bulimic sorority girls who were shoveling in another quick eight ounces at Yogurt Park. Telegraph Avenue, the main boundary between Commercial and Academic Berkeley, at dinnertime was a mass of starving young people. Great long strings of cheese extended from their mouths to the slice of Blondie's pizza held an arm's length away; desperate hands were digging into empty bags of gourmet naturelle cookies for a stray chocolate chip. Everyone was young and tan and handsome, licking, chewing, and sucking away. Little did they suspect: a Violator walked among them.

I picked up my dinner—a roll of root beer Life Savers. It was all I deserved. I was coming to traffic safety school for punishment. Oh sure, I wanted the ticket expunged from my record; I didn't want to build up four points in twelve months and stand to lose my license. Still, it was a bad deal moneywise. Traffic school costs twenty dollars for "tuition" plus ten dollars for court costs. Then, of course, there are the eight hours of your valuable time put in on two consecutive Monday nights—nights when you could be home compulsively working. On the other hand, the cost of failing to stop at Kittredge and Milvia streets is a mere thirty-five bucks. It really should be twenty bucks for me because, swear to God, *I stopped for a second. Look, Officer, you don't really need to go into first to stop, do you? I can stop in third. I've done it a million times.*

See, here's the truth: I speed. I rush around like a maniac all day. Whatever happened to the mellow hippie in me? Where is the woman who vowed to chew each mouthful of brown rice eight times before swallowing? She's gone '80s, that's where. She's doing forty on Martin Luther King Junior Way ("I have a nightmare . . ."). She's trying to sail nonstop through the downtown obstacle course. Do something, girl! You're a menace, I told myself. Go to the boring traffic safety school and sit there for eight hours and contemplate the stupidity of your ways. After all, the bottom line here is our old friends. Life and Death.

As I entered the Tan Oak Room of the University of California student union building, I was wondering just how the professor of trafficology would go about providing the guilt trip I craved. So imagine my shock when I saw the buffet, piled with platters of cheese chunks, fresh vegetable slices, crackers, and a huge plate of bean dip. The room was packed. People kept pouring in, looking first anxious then delighted as they helped themselves to the buffet. Was this to be my punishment? To be locked in a small room for four hours with one hundred people tanked up on refried beans?

It just didn't seem right—the tablecloth, the vase with one perfect yellow carnation, the apple juice, the sliced carrots and the cauliflower . . . but eventually I spotted an official-looking man walking through the crowd, passing out registration papers. A middle-aged black man with a goatee, he had the stage presence of a Shakespearean actor. Doctor of trafficology, I presume. I asked him if the buffet was provided by the school. No. "It was left from a previous class and nobody should be eating it," he said.

More people were piling into the room, helping themselves to the munchies. I asked those around me what they were in for. There were six people in my corner of the room alone who'd been caught speeding near the same intersection. The professor walked by, handing out more registration forms to the latecomers. I noticed him making a backhanded grab of a few chunks of jack cheese as he headed toward the door. "My goodness, look at all these violators," I said to the woman sitting next to me. "The streets aren't safe."

"They are tonight," she replied.

After about half an hour of filling out a three-line form, we tore into the curriculum: I. Defensive Driving; II. Safe Driving; III. Courteous Driving. ("When do we get to Paranoid Driving?" called out the first of many class clowns.) It was an eight-hour program that could be summed up in one message: Slow down, you aggressive, upwardly mobile, death-defying maniacs. The man with the goatee, Ted Bryant, taught the class while his partner, Robert Hempe, hung out, rewound film, and moved the buffet table out of the room. They told us they were "consultants for traffic safety." (Ever notice that three out of four people in university towns are consultants? Ask the guy in the big white hat with the green feather sitting in the red Cadillac what he does, and he'll probably say, "I'm an adult-entertainment consultant.")

Hempe and Bryant played the crowd like a team of cops. Bryant was the good guy, teaching us, listening to us, and presenting himself as a pleasant, reasonable man. Hempe, author of the *California Institute of Traffic Safety Workbook* (our text), was a bit more firm, occasionally injecting a defensive remark when the "question authority" crowd challenged the efficacy of the teaching methods. In his tight white slacks, the unsmiling Hempe resembled a shopping center Clint Eastwood.

We went over the questions in the workbook out loud. "How can we avoid violations?" was one. "Watch the rearview mirror," answered a class joker. "When do you drive the worst?" "When I leave my Seeing Eye dog at home," piped up another. "What are the greatest dangers on the road?" "Older people who shouldn't be driving," one young woman responded. (In fact there were only one or two people who appeared to be over fifty in the room. This crowd of bad drivers was predominantly of the white, male persuasion, generally in the twenty-to-forty age group. And if insurance rates reflect who drives the worst, then let's puncture the myths of the lady driver and the older driver right now. Rates are highest for adolescent males, then adolescent females, then all single males.)

In the course of the discussion Bryant tried to communicate certain rules of the road. Some emerged as clear and logical; others were inherently confusing. In commercial districts, we were told, U-turns are only permitted at controlled intersections; but some seemingly residential areas with apartment buildings are considered "commercial," so you can't U-turn freely on those streets either. (And don't try using driveways to turn around, because they are private property. We learned that drivers have been successfully sued by property owners who claimed their driveways were damaged by people who used them to turn around.)

The discussion seemed to be veering toward how to avoid tickets, rather than tackling the subject I was hoping for: What can we do about the fact we are all evil sinners? It was apparent that there were many MVs (multiple violators) in the crowd. At one point a woman began a question by saying, "This is my third time in traffic school," which caused uproarious laughter. Ted Bryant then asked for a show of hands from repeaters. We were looking at a 20 percent MV situation.

The number of times a person can cancel a ticket through traffic school in a given time period varies from county to county. Bryant said that the DMV (Department of Multiple Violators) has recently begun keeping track of how often you go to traffic school. A frantic voice called out, "When was that program started?" "First of last year," said Bryant. The anxious MV breathed a sigh of relief. At this point Robert Hempe (aka Clint Eastwood) came out of the woodwork to tell us that we can always go to court to ask the judge for more traffic school. "Here's how you do it," he said. "You say to the judge, 'I'd really like to go to traffic school. The community will be safer if I do. Please, may I have this opportunity?' "

We took a short break that lasted twenty-six minutes. As I stood in the hall talking to a group of fellow violators near the remains of the buffet, a bedraggled fellow came out of the elevator and looked at the table as if he'd just struck gold. He stuffed his satchel with vegetable slices and cheese chunks. The poor fellow appeared not to have had a bath in recent memory—in fact, he probably *had* no recent memory.

After the break we reconvened for what was to be the emotional highlight of traffic school: the showing of the movie *Red Asphalt II*. Bryant told us this film was the sequel to—you guessed it—*Red Asphalt*, the real-life horror film seen by millions of California youngsters in Driver's Ed. *Red Asphalt II*, he said, was an update.

"Newer bodies," quipped a classmate.

"Now, you don't have to look at it if you don't want to," warned Bryant. "And if you get woozy, don't get up, because you might faint." (Should Bryant ever decide to ditch trafficology, I think he has a future doing PR for MGM.)

The film is approximately twenty minutes of actual highway gore, shot at close range by CHPmen (as California Highway Patrol Police are known), stuff that makes De Palma and Peckinpah look like weak-kneed esthetes. Faces, heads, and bodies covered with blood, trapped in mangled vehicles. Bloody children, babies screaming. Close-ups of wounded motorcyclists—bones protruding through the gristle. Blood running from mouths, spilling into the gutter. All the while there is a loud rock sound track, interspersed with interludes of stiff-looking highway patrolmen reminding us of the grim facts that are truly at the heart of our culture: Accidents are the number one killers of the young; 40 percent of all traffic accidents involve the fifteen-to-twenty-four age group; if you stop on the highway for any reason, there is a significant risk of being hit by a drunk driver, and so on.

The film ends with an inside-the-morgue-drawer shot of the feet of a woman being pushed in. As the screen turns black you hear the CHPer turned grim reaper saying, "She made a mistake and now she has to pay. . . ."

Sorry to give away the ending, but I hope it will help you appreciate how emotional the film criticism session that followed became. Numerous women protested what they felt was the unnecessary sensationalism of the film. "It immobilizes you," said one woman. Hempe briefly stopped his noisy rewinding of the film to defend it. "The movie gives a police officer's point of view, the point of view of the person who has to pull the bodies out of cars."

Then we got a testimonial. "As a result of seeing this film," one guy said, "I now plan to wear seat belts." (Say hallelujah!) After a few more pledges from the Beltless Anonymous set, an angry young man felt compelled to speak. "I come from a state that outlaws the use of bloody films like these." (We later learned that the state in question is Michigan; apparently Motown powers don't like reminders of what their machines can do.) He said he'd learned traffic safety from charts and facts and claimed that, as a result, he's an excellent driver. (What was he doing in reform school?) He concluded by saying, "This proves that education is more important than cheap theatrics," to which one local yokel quipped, "But this is California."

The discussion went off onto a number of ideological side trips. In typical Berkeley style, Europe was held up as a role model, with one woman pointing to the superior wisdom of Europeans in mandating seat belts by law. To this a man replied, "In Europe they're used to being told what to do by kings and queens, but here in America where we love freedom, we wouldn't accept the DMV legislating seat belts." He also wanted it known—for the record—that "the leading cause of death for young black males is homicide." Things went on in this vein for a while until the instructor said, "I'm going to insist that we limit our discussion to traffic safety laws in California. Let's leave Europe and the rest of it out of this." Immediately a young woman raised her hand and said, "I want to say one more thing about Europe . . ."

Finally a frustrated woman spoke up. "I'm confused. I come to this film always wearing my seat belt, never drinking when I drive, and never getting under my car on the freeway. This just makes me more frightened than I already am. Why don't you follow up with a petition to make seat belts mandatory instead of a lot of hot air. . . ."

Finally we moved from defensive teaching to defensive driving, and learned more about how to fend off tickets. Generally, Bryant said, there is a five-mile allowance on speeding to allow for speedometer differences. "You're probably safe doing thirty on most streets," he went on. "The CHP are looking for changes in the traffic. They're not going after you because you drive a red Porsche or a yellow BMW—it's just that these people seem to want to move out from the flow of traffic."

At precisely 10:00 P.M., everyone bolted for the door. During the week between sessions, I experienced moments of heightened awareness while in traffic. I realized, for instance, that when in the pedestrian role, I hate the unyielding drivers who won't let me cross; but while driving, I resent stupid pedestrians who keep getting in my way. I realize that I drive more carefully when passengers are in my car. I made a concerted effort to remember to wear my seat belt and not to flash on scenes of blood-filled gutters. I'd guess I increased my seat belt usage by 50 percent, but I could only keep the blood flashes down in the daytime. Every night I saw those crying bloodied babies. It was no accident that I kept remembering the film. It provided the punishment I was looking for.

Reform School II began sans buffet. Ted Bryant gave us his theory of the Berkeley driver, attempting to explain why this small city has one of the highest accident rates in the state. "You have a lot of people coming here from back East who are not accustomed to allowing people to cross the street. Pedestrians have the right of way whenever they enter the street, but they are supposed to yield if they are endangering anyone." I imagined myself crossing a downtown street and yelling into the headlights of an oncoming red Porsche, "You from Jersey?"

The crowd at Night II was much more subdued, resigned to sitting through the four hours and getting their certificates. The wisecrackers didn't even bother. The atmosphere was akin to high school. Tonight people would fall asleep earlier, watch their watches more, and rhythmically twitch their legs for longer periods. The seats were so close together that I had to share in the pulsating foot-tapping of the woman on my left.

Most people had brought something else to do. These were the drivers who speed, pass on the right, roll to a sort-of-stop, weave through traffic to get ahead. They are going *Somewhere* with not a minute to waste. The man in front of me was working on his appointment schedule, a large notebook-size calendar. Under *Things to Be Done Today*, he had written: "Consider serving on ad hoc Computer Committee." He repeatedly flipped through previous *Things to Be Done Today*. In between "Vacation" and "Ski Trip" was "Call about traffic school." Next to him, a woman was reading *My Mother, My Self*. To my right, a lawyer-turned-journalist would whip through seventy-five pages of *The Light on Synanon* that evening. A jockish student was reading *International Finance*. Another woman in search of her self was reading *Self*. Down the aisle a central casting intellectual, complete with bow tie, was reading Jackie Collins's *Hollywood Wives*. I asked the lawyer-cum-journalist if he thought the bow tie was a visiting law professor from Harvard. "Not arrogant enough for Harvard," he observed. "Probably a professor of linguistics."

We learned more facts in a random sort of way: "Wanna hear something really weird?" a slightly spacy guy raised his hand and said. "Commercial plates can't park in ten-minute zones in San Francisco . . . that really blew my mind." (What can you say after you've said far fucking out?)

Bryant told us about new laws that mainly pertain to teenage drivers.

Item: Parents are now liable for $35,000 in damages if an accident is caused by their child who is under eighteen.

Item: A child with a 4.0 average in school can get significantly lower insurance rates.

Item: A child cannot get a license without the parent signing that he has observed the child for thirty hours of driving beyond Driver's Ed.

Bryant gave us more tips for dealing with the police. Besides being courteous, we should "admit to nothing." Don't say, "I wasn't doing forty-five, I was doing thirty-five"; instead say, "I realize I was going a little fast." Never give the officer information he hasn't asked for. Don't say, "But I've gone through there a hundred times," because then he'll know you've done it a hundred times. Finally, in a situation where radar is used, you have the right to request a readout.

At this point we took a break. Bryant had called out our names, and I was now paying the price for being a writer, "the eyes and ears of The People." A man sitting near me said, "Are you the writer? You know your last article . . . I didn't get it." Others came up to me and implored me to write the story of their ticket —usually a case of Incredible Injustice.

We returned from our break for the comic highlight of traffic school, a film titled *Under the Influence.* Here we were shown what purported to be a group of average people from Los Angeles who were "chosen for their proven ability to perform well under the influence of alcohol." The camera scanned the cross section of

Angelenos and we got a quip from each of them. We are talking about an average IQ of 67 max. They were to be trained to drive a course that included backing up through a zigzag path of red traffic cones. First they obtained a base score while sober; then they repeated the course after six drinks. "I think I drive better when I'm drinking. I'm less inhibited," one subject said. "I wanted to see what it would be like . . . free food, free booze," giggled another. Next we close in on a mascaraed, sultry San Fernando housewife. "Hi," she said in a breathy voice, "my name is Terry Lockey, but I prefer to be called Tree Lockey." Later we saw her, face expressionless, dead drunk, driving backward, smashing traffic cones and veering off course. The gentleman sitting next to me applauded and shouted, "Go, Tree baby!"

Instead of the heavy metal of *Red Asphalt II*, this flick came with a lively country-and-western sound track. It played while we watched these folks get, in their own words, "bombed . . . tipsy . . . intoxicated . . . drunk . . . snockered." It was as American as apple pie—the Dukes and Duchesses of Hazard. We saw them smiling and breathing into the "gas chromatograph," which proved their blood alcohol level had reached .10 percent, the legal definition of drunk. Then we watched as they demonstrated a 22 percent decrease in driving ability. We were reminded that 50 percent of all traffic deaths involve people who have been drinking. Unlike the horror of *Red Asphalt II*, the scenes of people getting bombed in this film were great fun to watch. As testimony to how ineffective this "fun" flick was, after seeing all these good old boys and girls whooping it up, I began to crave a gin and tonic.

The last hour of class was an orgy of toe-tapping, pencil biting, clock-watching and overt sleeping. Bryant was going over the answers to more workbook questions when, at exactly two minutes to ten, a woman cried out: "We have to go soon. I want my certificate of completion." Before he had a full-fledged mutiny on his hands, Bryant awarded us our diplomas. People grabbed them and rushed unceremoniously out of the room.

"You going on to college?" I asked my fellow passengers in the elevator. No one smiled. We were of two minds. There were the penitent among us who felt that we had done our time. And there were the unremorseful who felt they had been arbitrarily picked on while the *real* bad drivers were still on the road.

Walking to my car, I saw the bow tie.

"How was *Hollywood Wives?*" I asked.

"Not much," he said.

"What were you in for?"

"I'm a water consultant," he replied. "I consult for Asian governments, and I heard the king of Nepal was in town, so I was rushing to try to meet him."

"You see, Officer, I was speeding because I had to get to the king of Nepal."

"Sure, buddy, and I'm on my way to score some coke from Ed Meese."

Since my graduation I've been trying to change my nasty habits. I fade in and out of remembering to stay between twenty-five and thirty mph on city streets. I vow not to tailgate (definition: when you can't see the tires of the car in front of you touching the road). I frequently put on my seat belt. I ritually practice the zen of yielding.

And, inevitably, I think of *Red Asphalt II.* As sensational and even hokey as it was, it was the only part of the program that addressed the underlying reality that brought us there. It was akin to the little bag of real soybeans that sits on a table amongst the chaotic traders on the floor of the Chicago Board of Trade— the little chunk of reality that gets lost in the shuffle. I also remember a woman who once described to me what it was like to come upon the victim of a hit-and-run. "I held her in my arms as she bled to death. I was helpless."

We learned in traffic school that the most common causes of accidents are using alcohol, using pills or other drugs, driving in poor weather conditions, driving while fatigued, being careless, and speeding. During those intermittent moments of higher consciousness when I rise above my car/myself, and try to play by the rules, I become acutely aware of all the violators around me. I notice all the cars whizzing past me when I drive twenty-five, all the people crossing double yellow lines rather than stopping for pedestrians or other cars, all the horn-honking, unyielding, swerving, driven masses of humanity. They are people with Things to Be Done Today. They are going Somewhere. A drawer in the morgue is the last thing that comes to mind.

Another (Yawn) Orgasm Story

There may be a million yawn-orgasm stories in the naked city, but it was news to me. And I was determined to get to the bottom of it.

The facts are these: A friend sent me a clipping from *Omni* magazine alerting me to a tidbit of "Amazing Science" published in the august *Canadian Journal of Psychiatry* (vol. 28, pp. 569–570). It seems that three obscure clinical psychiatrists in the provincial town of St. John, New Brunswick, had inadvertently caught the attention of a Believe It or Not–hungry nation, but this story was true.

The Canadians had uncovered "Unusual Side Effects of Clomipramine Associated with Yawning." That was the title of their paper describing four patients who, while taking the antidepressant drug clomipramine (trade name: Anafranil) reported the unusual side effect of spontaneous orgasm every time they yawned.

The good doctors were alerted when one patient who had been markedly depressed for three months took the drug and—shazam! —"Complete symptom remission occurred within ten days."

Okay, she got over her depression awfully fast, but then she asked how long she would be "allowed" to continue the drug.

When the suspicious clinician questioned why she wanted to continue, the scientific paper reports, "She sheepishly admitted that she hoped to take the medication on a long-term basis, not so much because of the symptom relief that she had experienced, but rather because she had noted that since taking the medication, every time she yawned she had an orgasm. She found she was able to experience orgasm by deliberate yawning."

Think of the possibilities here. Imagine, if you will, a world in which "The Best of Carson" might become a stimulant!

A male patient, reporting similar symptoms, said that while he found the repeated climaxes "awkward and embarrassing, he elected to continue the medication because of the therapeutic benefit he obtained. The awkwardness and embarrassment were overcome by continuously wearing a condom."

A second male patient, however, less devoted to cure, discontinued the medication because "every time he yawned he experienced such an intense sense of exhaustion and weakness that he had to lie down for 10 or 15 minutes after each yawn."

Your reporter got on the case.

First I determined that there had been no reports of a run on Canadian pharmacies following the journal article. Further, there haven't been any reports of a rise in the number of patients complaining of symptoms of depression.

At Ciba-Geigy, the company that markets clomipramine in Canada and Europe, I was referred to a Miss Norekio, who monitors drugs for the firm. She explained that the drug is not available in the United States because the requisite number of FDA studies have not been performed.

"But hasn't the company been interested in exploring this unusual side effect?" I inquired by phone.

"I'm not the person to ask. I have no overall view of adverse experience with the drug on a worldwide basis," Norekio said in the careful manner of one who is speaking for a Big Company.

But faster than you can say Mike Wallace, I shot back, "Do you regard this as an *adverse* experience?"

"I don't know anything about it," she insisted when pressed for a response to the Canadian psychiatrists' report, ". . . but I did hear people in the elevator talking about it."

"The article wasn't intended to have a big response," says Dr. I. A. Kapkin, one of three authors of the journal report. "It was meant to alert clinicians to an effect that hadn't been reported." Speaking from his home in New Brunswick, Dr. Kapkin explained the genesis of his unusual paper:

"There is considerable yawning and sleepiness reported with antidepressants, but we had patients reporting, simultaneously, 'funny' side effects. We had to ask: 'What is funny?'"

"This is only observation, not research. It's a side effect, not a therapeutic effect," insists the appropriately cautious Dr. Kapkin, although a layman might argue that such a side effect is therapeutic.

"There was no suggestion to use the drug on sexual disorders," he says in response to my asking whether that possibility had been explored, ". . . although U.S. physicians have raised the question of using the drug for other purposes."

Dr. Lin Myers, who conducts research on impotence at Stanford University, notes that clomipramine did cause yawning in rats, although she was unaware of its causing orgasm. "There's been nothing on that besides the Canadian paper."

First, I inquire tactfully about how one knows a rat is yawning. "A rat just opens its mouth and yawns just like us, but they don't put their little paws up to their face."

Next I inquire how the phenomenon of orgasm is observed in rats, thinking for a moment that, in today's atmosphere of laboratory animal abuse, the lucky rat who lands in Dr. Myers's cage is in for a treat. "It hasn't been established yet that any female animal other than monkeys are known to orgasm," she said, alluding to a fellow scientist who got a grant from the National Institutes of Health to study orgasm in free-range female monkeys.

Dr. Myers, however, was able to cite research done at Stanford in which male monkeys were observed exhibiting "mounting behavior and erection" when given yohimbine, a tree bark extract that is known to be an aphrodisiac in rats. "In fact some guy in *Stamford,* Connecticut, opened up a storefront to sell yohimbine, calling it The Stamford Research Center. He put out a brochure showing smiling African natives with erections and quoted *Stanford* research on yohimbine. It got real sticky."

Dr. John Buffum, a research pharmacologist at the University of California–San Francisco and the author of a major review paper, "Pharmosexology: The Effect of Drugs on Sexual Function," said the Canadian journal report "stands out. There are no other reports of yawns and orgasms. I've never run across a reaction like that. There are other articles showing that it causes dysfunction," and in fact the same *Canadian Journal of Psychiatry* had published one such report a year before Kapkin et al. announced their findings to a bemused if not breathless world.

The question of how the antidepressant may lead to yawning and orgasm is one that has intrigued and eluded the scientists.

San Francisco psychiatrist Harvey Caplan, who specializes in sexual disorders, said, "There is a syndrome of when some people have orgasm they have fits of sneezing. And many people have a stuffy nose after orgasm.

"How that relates to yawning, I don't know. I guess all we can say is the head is connected to the genitals somehow," he said, laughing.

First yawning, now sneezing—there may be another story here.

"The only other slightly comparable report," notes Dr. Glenn Peterson, an Oakland psychiatrist, ". . . is of a type of epilepsy driven by photic stimulation—flashing lights, phone poles going by—that triggers an orgasmic response."

I leave it for other investigators to pursue this phenomenon.

Dr. Kapkin, who still doesn't understand why a few of his patients on clomipramine had this idiosyncratic response, thought it might be related somehow to endorphins in the brain. Endorphins are naturally produced opiate-like substances.

Says Kapkin, "The only similar phenomenon we know of is that, with opium withdrawal, people sometimes experience yawning and spontaneous orgasm." He referred to a letter published in the *Canadian Journal of Psychiatry* that followed his paper. Four New York doctors attempted to explain the yawn-orgasm effect in terms of a complex biochemical reaction associated with increased brain levels of the neurotransmitter serotonin. Clomipramine is known to act on serotonin levels.

Whatever the explanation, all agree that the yawn-orgasm patients' reports of complete remission of depression in ten to fourteen days are a bit unusual also. Says Dr. Peterson, "I don't know how you tie in an unusual sexual response with recovery—you don't have to produce multiple orgasms to get a complete antidepressant response. That would be an awkward kind of link."

Again it might be left to the layman to explain to the scientist why, under the circumstances, his patients were no longer depressed.

Interestingly, the company that might profit from such a link being made is uncomfortable with the research. Several people with whom I talked at Ciba-Geigy, who did not want to speak officially, expressed fear of sensational publicity over what is, after all, an unusual side effect. It occurred in a handful of people out of hundreds who have taken the drug.

It should also be noted that broader studies show that 26 percent of the males and 14 percent of the females using clomipramine reported adverse—truly adverse—effects on sexual performance.

Still, it is human nature to home in on the bizarre, the unusual, the funny sex story. Virtually everyone I know who saw the yawn-orgasm report was amused and wanted to know more. That's what prompted this investigation on everything you ever wanted to know about yawns and orgasm.

The only person who seemed indifferent was one friend who said of his wife of twenty-one years, "This is nothing new to us old, married people. My wife yawns every time she has an orgasm."

The Womanly Art
of Beast Feeding

Us parents, we have a hell of a time feeding our kids these days. How simple it was in the olden days when people knew nothing of the science of nutrition and the little darlings had to eat their porridge, swallow their spinach, and lap up their stew with its juices while keeping their yaps shut.

Today, it's not untypical to sit down to dinner and hear, "Oh, no, not steak again" or "I hate quiche Lorraine" or "Yuck—home-made tortellini with pesto." In my family, two girls, *tyrannicus girlus*, have divided up the known food world so that dining is virtually impossible. One hates Chinese, the other hates Mexican. One won't eat chicken, the other won't eat meat. They have achieved unity on fish and French cuisine—neither will eat either.

Concern about what the children eat naturally follows the returned importance of breast-feeding as fomented by those Friends of the Breast, the La Leche League. The League, which I always suspected grew out of the French obsession with the mammary gland (so evident in their art and their postcards), wrote a pamphlet, "The Womanly Art of Breast Feeding," which urged women not only to nurse their babies but to do it in public. They were aided in this effort by a male support group, the Le Lechers League.

It became gospel that a child who got off to a good start by consuming nothing but healthy breast milk would be hooked for life on simple natural foods. But has a truly scientific study ever shown that any child (or adult, for that matter) who spends long hours at the breast is any more intelligent for the experience?

Nevertheless, a generation of well-educated, busy women devoted themselves to breast-feeding. We nursed them in offices, we nursed them on buses, we nursed them at tax accountants except when the trauma made our milk dry up. Once I actually saw a bride come down the aisle nursing her baby. We pumped our milk and saved it lest we deprive our child while on the job. We bared our breasts as well-meaning fathers-in-law self-consciously shouted, "Chow bag!"

And what did we get for our effort? Offspring who, as soon as they could talk, demanded "Jell-O Pudding Pops—*now.*"

Well, we tried. Maybe we tried too hard. Maybe it's hopeless, in this crazy Ronald McDonald world, to think you can do something as simple as feed children well. Christ, I hardly know what to feed myself between low-fat, high-fiber, calcium-rich, iron-rich, nonadulterated foods. Vitamin pills, that's what most adults take to feel wholesome these days—pills.

There are several theories on how to handle the unmistakable lust for consuming junk that seems to be epidemic in our youth. There is the hard-line approach: Eat it and weep. Most of us parents are simply too wimpy for that. There is the bribery approach: Eat the chicken and vegetable and then you can have the cookies and ice cream and bubble gum. And finally there is the Little Bo-peep approach: Leave them alone and they will come home wagging their tails behind them.

The Bo-peep Plan or the non-nutrisystems approach allows the child to self-select foods. There have been scientific studies showing that if allowed to pick at random, a baby will eventually select all it needs to satisfy its nutritional needs. A similar approach can be taken with older children, but it is best done if the parent provides some structure. Here, some education is necessary so that the child can choose from the Seven Basic Junk Food Groups. A well-balanced meal would include something from each of the following:

THE SEVEN BASIC JUNK FOOD GROUPS

1. The Chip Group. Like any conscientious parent, I try to steer my little heifers toward the healthier chips—the pure, natural potato chip as opposed to cheese puffs or sour cream and onion. I skip barbecued anything. The children will enjoy exercising choice concerning the morphology of the chip—ruffled versus flat—as well as selecting among corn, potato, and the newer nacho chips that provide an opportunity to become aquainted with a different culture.

2. The Nitrate/Nitrite Group. There is a growing body of empirical evidence that children are born with an innate need for nitrates and nitrites. Whether it is due to a missing gene or a result of mutation is unclear. But no child's lunch is complete without the protein portion consisting of salami, bologna, bacon, hot dog, and so on. Further evidence of the biological need for nitrates is seen in the child's refusal to eat nitrate-free versions of these products amid claims that these adulterated foods taste "gross." Even children's normal intolerance of ambiguity in food is held in check as they select mysterious items like "luncheon meat."

3. The Grainless Bread Group. Thanks to modern marketing, a wide variety of grainless breads are now available, from the traditional Wonder to the historic San Francisco sourdough. And because of improved food technology one can even purchase a variety of whole wheat bread that is indistinguishable in flavor and texture from white. Don't ask me how they do it. No doubt some truth-in-labeling law requires that for every ton of processed flour one actual whole grain must be dropped in the mix. At any

rate, either bread will do very nicely to hold the catsup, mustard, or mayo that accompanies the nitrite filler.

4. The Fruitoid Group. Children quickly learn that there's a whole world of fruit-related products that are much sweeter and more interestingly packaged than actual fruit. These range from canned fruits that save wear and tear on teeth and jaws to fruit rolls in which the uninteresting pulp portion of the fruit is removed, leaving only the important sugar portion. This is arranged in a leathery substance that sticks to the teeth as well as the ribs. Since the addition of artificial fluorides have rendered much of modern dentistry unnecessary, these products are useful for restoring the natural balance between the tooth enamel and Mr. Cavity.

5. The Cake and Cookie Group. Although a balanced meal, one that includes all the basic junk food groups, makes it less difficult to get through the rest of the crap so one can come to the finale, the addition of a treat is always welcome. Most children prefer a sandwich-style cookie so the filling can be scraped off and the remaining cookie can still be traded with a friend for something else.

6. The Health Food Group. Most supermarkets now include a health food section where delicious snacks are displayed in large old-fashioned wooden bins to which you help yourself. Here one can find a variety of treats from plain carob chips to honey-soaked granola cereal (said to have nine times more sweetener than a Hershey bar). Some traditional foods here include the yogurt-covered nuts, and some stores even have mint-flavored yogurt-covered nuts. Those little bright green balls are my favorite natural food. To find out which ones your child likes, just have him reach in the bins, squeeze a few pieces, and eat a bunch of each one right out of his hands.

7. The Drink Group. Choosing a drink used to be a battle. Children always wanted Coke or Pepsi. But today's sophisticated kid is reaching out for natural-flavored soft drinks or oddities like cola-flavored Calistoga water. Exciting developments in fruit

drinks go beyond the traditional teeth-rotting apple juice to a whole range of drinks that boast of being fruit-flavored. One orange drink label brags "20% Real Fruit Flavoring!"

The wise parent will simply stand back and let the child choose among these groups. In fact, this is a process that may already be occurring in your house, but it's nice to read about it from an expert like myself so you can tell a friend that you saw an article saying it was okay to do this.

IV

Bored in the U.S.A.

All in a Day's Work

Why does all this startling, bizarre, and sensational stuff about Marilyn Monroe and the Kennedy boys keep coming out? I can't tell if it's a Republican plot to insure that Teddy never runs or a Democratic plot to remind us of what manly rascals, what little dickenses, that JFK and his brother Bobby were. Someone seems bent on taking us back to the glory that was *Shtupelot*.

One beneficiary of the ongoing drama historians will perhaps call *The Kopechniad* ought to be poor Jackie O-FK. When I read the gory—and I'll get to the *really* gory stuff soon—details of these relationships I can't help but wonder about those Washington wives. Were Jackie and Ethel aware? Did they have to be pressured into shutting up? Or did they have a little hunk or two on the side themselves?

While reading Anthony Summers's book, *Goddess: The Secret Lives of Marilyn Monroe*, I was particularly struck by a remark attributed to Monroe by a friend. To wit, MM supposedly complained that JFK was in too much of a hurry for foreplay. Doesn't that make you just want to stand up and shout: *Men!* And think of poor Jackie—no foreplay, no afterglow, she hardly even got the Big Payoff.

I fear this kind of important information will be used against us women by busy men all over the world. "Listen, if it was good enough for Marilyn Monroe, it's good enough for you, tootsie. Three minutes, start to finish—take it or leave it." Well, slam, bam, and thank you masked man.

But when it comes to invasion of privacy, the chapter from the book that really takes the cake is the one describing famed L.A. coroner Thomas ("Coroner to the Stars") Noguchi's autopsy on Monroe. The day I was sitting in the office coffee room reading it, I said to an associate who caught me, "This is absolutely the most disgusting thing I've ever read." And I simply couldn't stop.

The autopsy episode discussed the search for the evidence of foul play based on the hypothesis that Monroe was murdered, rather than a suicide. Numerous scenarios were offered giving a motive for murder. The Kennedys themselves may have wanted to silence Monroe because she knew too much, was pregnant by one of them, or was about to create a scandal by going public with the whole affair. Another theory was that the Mafia did it to get back at the Kennedys. If you spent your youth in Greenwich Village basements listening to Mark Lane raise the national paranoia clock to near midnight, this way of thinking becomes perfectly logical when dealing with Kennedys and conspiracies.

Everyone agrees that Monroe was suicidal and that she did in fact die of an overdose of barbiturates. The problem (and bait for conspiracy theorists) lies in the absence of evidence that the barbiturates were consumed in capsule form. No capsule dye was ever demonstrated. This suggests the lethal dose was administered by either injection or—hold on to your seats—enema! Yuck. The plot sickens. It's bad enough that we've been on a voyage to the center of Ronald Reagan's colon, now we have newspapers all over the country describing in detail the appearance of Marilyn Monroe's anus twenty-two years after the poor soul is dead and gone.

Even more startling to those of us not in the autopsy business is the quote from Noguchi about his search for needle marks that would support the fatal-injection theory. He stated he inspected her arm veins and her tongue. Okay, I can live with that. But then, as readers of family newspapers all over the country learned, Noguchi announced he carefully inspected her vagina—with a magnifying glass.

Now, let us just imagine the scene in the Noguchi home that evening. Tom Noguchi, weary from a long day in the lab, comes home. He throws his trench coat and his magnifying glass on the hall tree and calls out, in his customary manner, "Honey, I'm home."

His wife—let's suppose she is one Marge Noguchi—steps out from behind the swinging kitchen door with a large casserole of hamburger Stroganoff in her hands. She leans over and gives him the customary peck on the cheek. "Just in time for dinner. I hope you washed up."

"I always wash before leaving. You know that, sweetheart."

Already seated at the family dinner table are eleven-year-old Kitten Noguchi and her sixteen-year-old brother Buzz. "Hi, Pop," shouts the strapping youngster. "Glad you're home, I'm famished."

As she is passing the noodles au gratin, Marge Noguchi asks her husband the usual question: "So how were things at the office today?"

"Oh, the same old stuff . . . a few gunshot wounds, a couple stabbing victims. There was some kind of minor gang war in East L.A. Later on, we had a guy with a massive coronary. Wow. We pulled a hunk of cholesterol out of him that would stop up the Colorado River. Oh, yes, and I spent the entire afternoon looking at Marilyn Monroe's vagina."

Marge Noguchi straightens up in her chair. "Um, Kitten, do you think you could go in the kitchen and get a few more biscuits? And, Buzz, this salad is really skimpy. How about going out back and picking up a few dandelion greens?"

The youngsters, who are well brought up, immediately appreciate their mother's serious tone and obey. As soon as they are out of earshot, Marge looks Tom in the eye and lets him have it.

"I thought I told you never to bring up Monroe's vagina at the dinner table."

"But, honey, you asked what I did."

"Don't you have any brains? Don't answer that! Couldn't you think about how this might affect Buzz and especially Kitten?"

Tom Noguchi throws down his napkin in disgust. "Boy, this is what I get for sharing my life with you. Women! As the old saying goes: can't live with 'em, can't kill 'em."

The next day, on the way to junior high, Kitten Noguchi is chatting with her best friend, Cookie Fong. "Well," Kitten purrs, "my dad is like so totally, totally gross you wouldn't believe it . . ."

"Sure, I would," says Cookie, cracking up. "My dad like is getting hairs in his ears. I mean that is so gross, just sooo radically gross . . ."

Meanwhile, in a parking lot outside Hollywood High, Buzz Noguchi is bragging while tossing a football to his best friend, Kent Ortega. ". . . And that's just one of the things my pop did at the office," he says boastfully.

"Wow, it would really be boss to be a coroner," says Ortega. "Say let's get together after school and practice calculus."

My Neighborhood, My Self

It's a typical day in my neighborhood, a place Mr. Rogers might call the Land of Make-believe. The streets are coming alive with people of all ages who seem to have been frozen in their early thirties. The Volvos and Datsun wagons and vintage VW bugs are flying up Cedar Street as if the drivers had never learned to meditate. The homeless people are crawling out of the bushes behind the Co-op market and the Safeway store and packing up their sleeping bags. The sous-chefs at Chez Panisse are chopping chanterelles, although the restaurant will not open for dinner for another nine hours. It's not a typical neighborhood, but mine own. Or maybe it is typical of the gentrified, upscale neighborhoods of the '80s.

I've been walking these streets so long, kvetching the same old song, I know every crack in these dirty sidewalks of Shattuck. North Berkeley—my home, my self—is well known for its food businesses, particularly Chez Panisse, the Cheeseboard, the Co-op, and Peet's Coffees, but there's more going on in these streets, things more strange and more mundane. I am a prisoner of shopping here, unable to leave Berkeley for fear of going through violent coffee and baguette withdrawal. I have succumbed to the community fetish of freshness.

I've heard that you can tell Democrats from Republicans by the way they shop. Democrats go to the supermarket once a week. Republicans go to small shops every day. North Berkeley's made a Republican out of me.

About once a week, though, I democratically make my pilgrimage to Peet's Coffees for a pound of Guatemalan, ground for Melitta. On this sunny morning, people are swarming in front of the shop for the A.M. fix. You can tell the regulars because they bring their own ceramic mugs. Peet's at nine-thirty is the closest thing to a community this neighborhood has.

Today, every outside bench is taken. The stairs on the church across the street are packed. People hold up Styrofoam cups in homage to the fresh-roast gods. The baby-boomlet moms gingerly steer their umbrella strollers through the gauntlet of cupholders. Over by the *Express* box a woman is telling her friend a dream. "This guy who really fucked me over a couple of years ago comes up to me and asks to borrow a pencil. When he loses it I say to him, 'How long can you continue to betray people's trust in you?'"

People on the streets around here still smile at you and say, "Hi," like they did in the '60s, but they no longer say, "Have a nice day." Up at the Bank of America I see a man who was a cause celeb—a radical leader who once called for "direct action" —making a withdrawal from the Versateller machine. Standing in the long line at the French Hotel Café is a world-famous performance artist who returned from Europe this year because he missed North Berkeley. These streets are crawling with writers, artists, activists, and others who've been famous for more than fifteen minutes.

The "bread line" to buy fresh baguettes has not yet formed outside the Cheeseboard, though the spare-changers are beginning to work the street. The smell of baguettes a-bakin' makes it difficult to walk around without feeling hungry. Soon, Richie will set up his Livermore Action Group table in front of the store. He's my six-year-old's favorite neighborhood character. I always imagine her singing the Sesame Street song "Who Are the People in Your Neighborhood?" this way: "The peace-button guy's a person in my neighborhood, in my neighborhood . . ."

A woman sits on a bench in front of the Bank of America eating a bran muffin and reading *Major Trends in Jewish Mysticism*. Perhaps she is one of the people who attends the Melia Center across the street. The Melia Center advertises that it offers "an exploration"—not a class, not a workshop, but an exploration— called "The Soul of Jewish Mysticism." In fact, the Melia Center turns out to be one of five educational institutions on this block. Tucked into the middle of the block is the Acupressure Workshop, where you can release shoulder and neck tension in two and one half hours. (If that fails, you can always pick up "a pint of shoulder pads" at La De Da.) Also on the block are the Center of Intuitive Arts, the Synergy Power Institute, and the Jungian Dreamwork Institute. Perhaps the pundits who dubbed this "the gourmet ghetto" have missed the point. It's really the fringe-o institute ghetto.

Despite this obvious major trend, the block owes its national fame and its parking problems to the little restaurant behind the redwood fence and the monkey puzzle tree. On this morning, the chefs in the Chez Panisse kitchen are busy preparing things like potato and chanterelle gratin, pigeon salad, butternut-squash ravioli, red and yellow tomato salad with tarragon mayonnaise and nasturtiums, and white chocolate mousse with *fraises de bois*.

The restaurant staff is an attractive group of young, enthusiastic men and women who appear to have as much mousse in their hair as they have on the dessert menu. This institution has perfected a style of cuisine that can only be described as oral compulsive. Much of its success can be attributed to chef-leader Alice Waters, who has probably combined creative and entrepreneurial skills more than any other woman in the country. She is also the author of the best-read piece of literature in town. Even at 9:00

A.M. a line is forming to read the menu that is posted outside Chez Panisse.

The intellectual equivalent of Chez Panisse is just up the street and provides what passes for nightlife in North Berkeley—Black Oak Books. While other neighborhoods have bars (North Berkeley does have a very nice one—Moriarty's—but it's also, of course, a restaurant), Black Oak is the place to go after hours, which in this neighborhood means when the Produce Center closes. The selection is tasty and ranges from literary chanterelles like Céline to Big Macs like Garfield. Most people are surprised by the beauty of the bookstore. The large, airy rooms with natural wood everywhere turn out to be a side effect of making the place livable for the highly allergic group who work there. Even though the area is known for opposing new businesses, Black Oak became a neighborhood institution in a matter of months. And that's nothing to sneeze at.

But as night falls in North Berkeley most people migrate to the bizarre oasis of Bill's Drugs. You never know who you'll see there. On a recent evening I ran into the schoolboard-president-cum-torch-singer and former-leftist-cum-Mohawk-coiffed-rightist Eldridge Cleaver. They were not together.

There may be other stores that belong to the Outside World in this neighborhood—businesses like Mary's Place and Sale's Barber Shop and Beauty By Grace and University Hardware and Plumbing, which looks as if it hasn't had a customer since Hoover was in office. But Bill's is where we all—we of the food-perfecting and intellectual-gourmandizing set—go to mainline America.

When I want to venture back to the America of my childhood, I go to Virginia Bakery. When I want to bring back the '60s, man, I go to Smokey Joe's Café. When I want to see people work hard for the money, I go to Owl Shoe Repair. But when I want to put my finger on the pulse of that big, bad kulture out there, I walk around Bill's Drugs and see what this country is on.

A survey of the end-aisle specials at Bill's reveals the following drugs: special Old Brussels cheese waferettes, Royal no-bake

lemon meringue pies, Wine Cooler of California, Weight Watchers mayo, Hand Launch aircraft replicas, Voltron Defender of
the Universe sticker books, Contempra indoor electric Char-B-
Que, Metamucil (regular or orange), pain reliever w/o aspirin,
Smurf vitamins, Massengill Scent of Country Flowers disposable
douche, and new Dip 'n Eat sauce for chicken. The juxtaposition
of the products is staggering: cat food next to Castrol GTX motor
oil, Tucks pads next to Ragú spaghetti sauce, Cara Mia artichoke
hearts next to binders, and so on. All of this—the whole panoply
of schlock—is displayed in a huge series of aisles illuminated by
enough fluorescence to make anyone's face appear dotted with
paisleys. I hope nobody ever walks into Bill's actually *on* drugs.
There is major freak-out potential here.

Most people probably don't appreciate the fact that North
Shattuck is also a kind of mini financial center. Despite the pau-
city of pinstripes, some of the mini-est financial institutions in the
world are located here. There're Cal American Savings, First En-
terprise Bank, and Homestead Savings. None of these are threat-
ened with acquisition by T. Boone Pickens.

There were once stores in this neighborhood I miss now, stores
that were here for years before the trendies scouted it out. There
was Sally G's shoe repair, where the tough-as-leather Sally always
gave my child a balloon. There was the pseudo-drugstore in the
old Poulet shop where the neighborhood geezers sat at the soda
fountain drinking beer. But most of all, I miss the old Vine Variety, replaced by Cocolat. With its wood floor, its notions and dry
goods, its toys and housewares, it was the sweetest spot around.
Halloween never seems like Halloween without Vine Variety.
You can keep the Chocolate Decadence. Give me a harmonica
made out of chewable orange wax.

Still, the changes have made it possible to walk these streets day
after day and never get bored. The endless stream of characters
through the neighborhood is my bread and butter. Sometimes I'll
be looking in the window glass of a store, staring at the reflection

of some weirdo and having a good laugh at said weirdo's expense. Then, suddenly, it hits me. The weirdo is me.

Maybe it's time I got out, headed north, someplace different. Anyone for Marin County?

Legacy of the Oval Bed

In time, the world will forget the Ayatollah, Ron, and Ollie Shaw and Ronald Reagan certainly won't be remembered as the president who balanced the budget or achieved arms control—or even recriminalized abortion. The world will little note nor long remember that he went to Bitburg, admired Rambo, and conquered Grenada. However, when he survived cancer surgery and said, "Nancy Reagan is my everything," we got a glimpse of how this presidency has distinguished itself.

It is possible that the Reagans are the first couple in history to actually get it on in the oval bed.

Think about it. Has there been a president in recent history whom we can imagine making the primal scene? Can we picture any president giving the executive order to his first lady other than this seventy-six-year-old stud who calls his wife "Mommy"?

Now, Jack and Jackie projected an image of attractive sensuality, but, the nation's finest investigative reporters have been telling us for years, Mrs. Kennedy was more like his fifth lady. She's said to have stood in line somewhere after Marilyn, Kim, Sam Giancana's mistress, *ad T&A infinitum*. Bobby, although reputedly Jack's equal as a lady's man, at least gave Ethel the time of day.

It's nearly impossible to imagine LBJ going all the way. Lyndon Baines's whole style was pubescent. We can sooner imagine him flipping the bird than romancing the Lady Bird. This, after all, is the man who tried to make his postoperative paunch into a national sex symbol. I think it was fairly obvious that the man sublimated all his sexual energy into trouncing deer with his Cadillac on the banks of the Pedernales.

As for Richard "Tricky Dickie" Nixon, let me say this about that. Despite his obsessions while in office, he was a decent husband, no doubt. He probably saw that Pat had everything she wanted short of a fur coat and a good time.

Nixon's whole style was that of "a man's man"—kibbitzing with Haldichman all day, mixing his special martinis for Bebe and Vesco all night, playing cards until his cash and energy ran out, sending his henchmen to look in the back of Daniel Ellsberg's brown slacks for spare change.

Of course, in those days Pat Nixon wasn't exactly a sizzling little enchilada herself. I'd guess the best the Nixons ever did while in the White House was a modified limited hang-out.

Jerry Ford, no doubt, tried, but the poor man had as much savoir faire as an English muffin.

"Is that it, Betty?"

"Nope. But close."

"How about there?"

"Higher."

"There?"

"Lower . . ."

Crash! Bam! Kerplunk!

"Okay, Jer. No touchdown tonight, Big Fella. Now get up off the floor and go to sleep."

Jimmy Carter might have made a great First Husband, but he had a tragic flaw. He was held hostage by lust. He was so busy lusting after other women in his heart that there was nothing left for Miz Rosalynn but peanuts. But that was okay. It was the era of limits.

You see my point. The more you look at history—the more you think about Eleanor and Franklin and Whoever, the more you get into who liked Ike and whether there was life under Mamie's pillbox—the hotter the Reagans look.

Since Jack Anderson wasn't alive to chronicle it, we'll never even know the sleazy truth about Rachel Jackson or Hannah Van Buren or Lucretia Garfield or Ida McKinley and the endless tales of longing buried in the linen on Pennsylvania Avenue.

The current regime, however, has left its image—that of the contented cowboy and his lady in red. Someday, when we're all old and wanting geriatric porn, we'll rush to the video shop for *President and Mrs. Reagan*—the movie.

California Drifting
and Other Roadside Attractions

As you travel the highways and byways and freeways and strange ways of this great golden state of ours, as you visually snort that white line of roadway, as you yell at your children, "Shut up or I'm leaving you here in Yuba City"—you may perhaps take some time out to wonder: Who creates all the signs for stupid Californians? You may also wonder, tangentially—because the highway offers endless tangents—what it is that drives writers mad on a hot summer day with the metaphors sizzling in their brains like mesquite on a witch's hibachi. You may ask, "What is it?" and still go make your visit.

Still, as you fly through the road with the greatest of ease and burn that gas that seems cheap by comparison as you think about how we brought that goddamn OPEC to its knees, as you think about how gasohol was part of Carter's plans to turn Americans into conservers (conservers! Jesus saves, Americans don't have to) —as you're moving right along, you might stop all this tangential thinking and return to the cruel myth of the stupid Californian. Genus: *Californiac.* Species: *stupidicus.* Common name: airhead. I'm not sure where this vicious lie began. My friend Dobby is certainly a leading exponent of the rumor continually describing his bicoastal childhood this way: "Every time I moved back East, I was behind in school and ahead in sex."

I, personally, do not consider the Californian any more stupid than the next dumb American—or even dumb European, for that matter. I blame a certain part of the bad rep on the California accent, that colorless, accentless, odorless, tasteless monotone. It's not just Valley Girls who talk that way—it's valley boys in pickup trucks and middle-aged coastal women driving dirty black Porsches and perfectly respectable San Mateo investment counselors wheeling spotless silver LeBarons. They really, really can't totally help it. It's not their fault that they didn't learn Midwest chattiness or East Coast motor-mouthing. They are not stupid. They just talk with that stupid accent.

Yet, as you roam the back roads and four-wheel the dirt roads and wind-skate the boardwalks of Alta California, you may get the impression that the sign makers in the state are assuming a certain beta-minus mind as the norm. These signs are an insult to us California intellectuals, we who read *Doonesbury* and watch *Masterpiece Theater* and like to argue endlessly about quality-time food. (After all, what is it that binds Berkeley together but the assumption that we alone are the brains of the state, the book people, the conscience of the unconscionable pleasure zone?) Let me offer here as evidence a few examples that I have collected of these affronts to the frontal lobes of our citizens. Maybe you have others.

Last spring as I crossed a bridge over the troubled waters near Calaveras County, I came upon exhibit A. It was a long span across the New Melones Reservoir and at the deepest point, I'd guess a sixty-foot drop, a sign said: NO JUMPING OFF BRIDGE. Now, clearly, no one who was not seriously bent on suicide would have considered even *leaning* off that bridge. I can only assume the sign writers felt that some stupid Californian would drive up and say, "Oh, shit. I drove all this way and now I'll have to drive back and use the Golden Gate like every other suicide victim. Just my luck."

Recently I saw Ms. Whoopi Goldberg holding down a parking place in front of McDonald's. (Broadway, Hollywood, Cary Grant walking in her dressing room and saying, "Whoopi, Whoopi, Whoopi," and she still can't pay someone to hold her parking place.) It turns out she was escaping from the Spielberg compound above Universal City, where she is being forced to film *The Color Purple* and eat health food at the same time. After so many Mac attacks, the Whoop finally escaped from L.A. County to come eat the meat of home. She did report, however, that while trolling L.A. for junk food she came upon the following primo example of a sign for stupid Californians. It was in the window of the La Brea International House of Pancakes that the words WE NOW HAVE MENUS IN BRAILLE! appeared.

Exhibit C came my way in the cosmopolitan but possibly genuinely stupid town of San Diego. What a weird place that: bums on the beach, people sleeping under dumpsters, Telegraph Avenue by the sea. No wonder someone on the San Diego State University campus felt obliged to put up a BOOTH CLOSED sign at the campus parking lot entrance booth.

Now, get the scene. It's winter break. The campus is a ghost town. There is not one little dune buggy or Subaru Brat in the huge parking lot of this drive-through campus. I walk through and see the sign. I imagine some SDSU student driving up and carrying on a long conversation with the booth until he notices the sign. "Oh, I'm sorry. You're closed. Forgive me for bending your ear. I better go over to the gas station and let some air out of my head."

My pal Dobby, the one of bicoastal childhood fame, has as his unenviable task the higher education of stupid Californians. He teaches literature and writing at Davis, an outback campus of the University of California. You know what I mean? He has to commute to the legendary valley of the dummies. On the way, he frequently passes a sign with a blinking red light that says TURN ON LIGHTS WHILE FLASHING. Here, we can imagine a long line of well-lit guys in trench coats, turning on their headlights and yelling, "Yoo-hoo, lady!"

Exhibit E, as in editor, is offered by my friend and editor John Raeside. When I discussed doing a signs-for-stupid-Californians in-depth report, Raeside offered his favorite. (And what editor can resist putting his two cents in an especially dumb story?) Here goes—my editor's favorite stupid sign for equally moronic Californians: WEAVE.

You've seen it. Down near San Jose where Highway 17 suddenly throws you a one-way ticket to Palookaville (aka L.A.). Many lanes converge, and the sign graphically depicts this as a bunch of dotted lines meeting and then the simple syllable—say it out loud and it's almost like praying—WEAVE. I suppose the guys over in the Caltrans sign division were having a couple of brewskis one day and studying the highway map.

Sign maker 1: Hey, Two, get a load of this. What do we call it?

Sign maker 2: I call it a genuine fucking mess, buddy. I say we just post that spot: GFM.

Sign maker 1: Oh, come on, you can't talk that way in public. Wait. I got it. How about: WING IT.

Sign maker 2: Too brutally honest. Let's just say WEAVE and see if we get any survivors.

I suppose this is not quite the incontestable evidence, the brilliant reduction ad absur-*dumb* argument I envisioned when I began my research for this project several years ago. Rather than making a case for the allegedly stupid Californian, I have either laid the groundwork for my own readmission to the third grade (a recurring nightmare of mine in which I can't fit in the little desk) or I have merely presented another Platonic toy, a dancer from the dance debate. To wit: It may not be the Californian who is stupid so much as the California sign maker or, perhaps, stupidity is in the dunce cap of the beholder. Which reminds me, for no logical reason but for mere tangentialist cheap thrills, of the first time I saw a sign and said to myself, "Now there's one you won't see in Omaha."

The sign in question was an amateur job, placed on a moving vehicle by the driver. The day we saw it was a sunny day on the San Diego Freeway in the smoggy, silly heart of L.A. I was with my friend Max, who had the common habit of yelling out insults to the other cars on the freeway, incurring the risk of a punch in the nose but usually just getting off with the Finger. At the time of this particular sign-sighting, Max had just released a string of French curses at a Mercury Marquis, a car he addressed as, "Hey, Marquis—Marquis de Sade!"

But even mad Max clammed up as the Cadillac drove by. It was a 1960ish mint condition, white convertible with maximum tail fin expansion. At the wheel was a tall, bare-chested black man, his wrists clad in studded leather, his height enhanced by a large white Stetson hat with a long chartreuse feather stuck in the band and now blowing in the wind. Seated beside him was a sexy red-head in a sequined halter. As they drove by the man looked at me and laughed exuberantly. When they passed us, I saw the sign on the back of the car, plastered across the trunk, foot-high letters: I MARRIED A WHITE WOMAN. Obviously he was concerned that some stupid Californian might not appreciate that his intentions were honorable. *Married* was the key word here; he was not just screwing the white woman.

Now, many people criticize Californians for their casual sharing of the intimate details of their lives. They view this openness as further proof of stupidity. They do not understand. We are on the cutting edge, where the personal becomes the moving vehicle. So, take me to the highway, show me those signs. Isn't California just the limit? I think I'll head out with my car posted DRIVER CARRIES NO INTERNAL MEMORY.

A Night in the Suburbs

I'm not sure when I began to define residents of suburban America as "them"; it was probably around the early '60s, around the time I first learned the word *bourgeois* and how to say it with stylized adolescent contempt. Prior to that, however, I would have said that the suburbs were my goal.

I remember the first time I saw one. It was 1956, and my friend Sharon had moved from our Chicago neighborhood to Homewood Heights or Township Park or Highland Manor—something like that. I had never seen streets so clean, so orderly, so perfectly uniform. Each house had a driveway and a garage and a lawn. Many even had their own swing sets—which I viewed as the ultimate. Everything for miles around was brand-new and, of course, there were the pastel colors everywhere.

Today, when young people talk about the '50s as if it were some lost golden age, those of us who came to consciousness in that era and remember its repression and conformity may be stunned. But when I remember how that suburb looked to me back then, I know what they are nostalgic for—a more hopeful time when we built new homes and ate off pink Melmac plates and drank from chartreuse metal tumblers.

I was thinking about this as I drove through the Caldecott Tunnel, our link to the suburbs, last week. Why was I driving to the suburbs to participate in a discussion on the topic of "nuclear war and what I can do to stop it"? Certainly not because I believe I can. And not even because it makes me feel better to try. Perhaps it was just because my interest in suburbs is just as keen as it was many years ago.

I had been invited to this evening's activities by my friend Russ. He had told me about how he and his wife, Pat, had become involved with a new group called "Beyond War." He described it as a nationwide organization consisting of people who were horrified at the prospect of nuclear war and who wanted to discuss alternate forms of national policy. "We start from the premise that war is obsolete," he had said. Apparently the goal is to develop ways to influence the nuclear powers by meeting in small groups in homes across America. Was this the beginning of Suburbanites for Social Responsibility?

Emerging from the tunnel, I drove past Orinda, the first of many well-planned towns. Ahead, Mount Diablo, the highest peak in these hills, came into view like a spectacular backdrop for a western. Exiting in Lafayette, Russ's town, the first thing I noticed when I hit downtown was the office of Congressman Ron Dellums, one of the most antiwar congressmen in history. Then I saw a sign in a store window that announced in eighteen-inch black bold letters: MESQUITE CHARCOAL. You call this the suburbs? I guess we really are all brothers and sisters after all.

I followed the detailed directions down winding roads with jogging paths, kids on bicycles, hiking trails, and maybe even some horses nearby. Beautiful green trees dotted the straw-colored hills. There seemed to be as many school-crossing signs as stop signs. At the end of a lane was Russ and Pat's house, right smack up against the rolling hills.

Russ showed me around a modest house that, while certainly lacking the luxury of an older home in the Berkeley hills, is a comfortable family home; it's just the kind of place I dreamed of in 1956. There was really only one detail Russ wanted to show me on his property. He slid open the patio doors and pointed to the hills that rose up sharply from his backyard.

"We wanted to have this for the kids to play in," he said of his piece of the Contra Costa hills. Recently, however, his son had been up there playing with a friend, and a rattlesnake bit the playmate. The child survived, but playing in those hills will never again be the carefree luxury the parents who bought homes nearby had envisioned.

Maybe that's what this story is all about: the rattlesnake in the backyard, the nightmare of nuclear war that has disturbed the tranquillity of suburban life. This was a for-the-children crowd, I soon learned as we gathered in Russ and Pat's living room, explaining why we were there to talk about nuclear war. We went around the room and introduced ourselves. Our leaders for the Beyond War orientation program were Roger and Judi, a financial planner and ex-teacher respectively, the parents of two boys. Roger and Judi looked like sportswear models—tan, attractive, in tennis-three-times-a-week good shape. Judi explained that she became concerned about nuclear war when her friend who teaches high school English described the depressing essays about "Life in the Future" he got from his students. "Only one essay was positive," Judi said, "and when the teacher asked this child why, she said that even though she knew her friends were worried about nuclear war, she wasn't. 'Because my parents are doing something about it.'"

The other couples seated in the cozy, low-ceilinged room reiterated this need to give the children hope. There were Al and Verna, an architect and his wife who have four children. Verna said, "You hear about teenagers using drugs and committing suicide because they have no hope for the future." Another couple, Pete and Jaynese, described themselves as "Berkeley radicals who moved to the suburbs but listen to public radio all day." Jaynese added, "I'm worried for my family, but I have my own dread. I've felt on the fringe in the past, estranged from my government."

There were two women there without husbands. One of them, Marsha, sat next to me hemming a dress and not saying much. (The next day she told Russ she had been so disturbed by the program that she had had a hard time getting to sleep.) Russ said he was there because while he would like to deny the possibility of nuclear war, his experience as a member of Physicians for Social Responsibility made denial impossible. Pat said of her two kids, "They ask me about nuclear war. They talk about it. That disturbs me."

The evening consisted mostly of a prepared presentation delivered by Roger and Judi. They had obviously undergone some kind of Beyond War leadership training and used printed charts and materials from a Beyond War orientation kit. Roger stood next to a large photo he had brought of the earth and explained, in an upbeat tone, that he was here to show us that there is hope. "We're not talking about protesting or lying down in the streets or anything like that. We're not a fringe group; we're middle Americans."

We adjourned to the den to watch part of a cassette on *The Last Epidemic*. Interestingly, when Roger switched off the VCR, there was a special on nuclear war on the TV news station. Then Roger went through a series of exercises designed to dramatize the reality of our current megatonnage. He had us close our eyes while he dropped pebbles in a mental garbage can. These represented the strike power of our current Trident and Poseidon arsenals. As I opened my eyes and focused on the copy of *Cosmos* by Dr. Carl Sagan on the bookshelf, Roger was asking, "How did that impact you?"

Then we watched another cassette. This one featured the ubiquitous Dr. Sagan describing the phenomenon of "nuclear winter," the catastrophic effects on the earth from the global temperature changes that would follow even a limited nuclear war. After this depressing clip Roger said, "I don't know how that impacted *you*, but the first time I saw it, I was devastated." His wife, Judi, who had also seen the program several times before, looked as if she was about to cry.

Frequently during the evening, prosaic images of ordinary suburban life would be used to make a point. For example, when Roger was talking about the imperative to survive, he said, "Anyone who's ever pulled a weed out of a driveway knows what a survivor is like." When Judi talked about overcoming the feeling of inertia and hopelessness people have, she said, "If we can have a successful marriage, we can change countries."

Still, after nearly three hours of listening, I failed to see what Beyond War was offering. The group discussions were touching and meaningful, but Roger was frequently so intent on going through the prepared spiel, he didn't perceive that the group was already ahead of him. Everyone agreed that a nuclear war is not survivable or worth surviving. They also, I think, believed that it is in the interest of the United States and the Soviet Union to maintain the current world order. Some expressed concern about the wild cards—Khomeini, Qaddafi, Israel—what can we do about the fact that the nuclear genie is out of the bottle in a world of people with beliefs they will die for?

As Roger was going through the charts from Beyond War, I had a strange flashback to a day in my childhood when Christian missionaries came to our neighborhood park. They were ladies in summer dresses and big floppy hats who asked if we could take Jesus into our hearts. Somehow, Beyond War had the feeling of an end-of-the-world cult—a new, strange, fin de siècle religion. But then, perhaps a new religion is what is needed after all, an antinuclear fanaticism to compete in a world of strong beliefs.

Although Roger's presentation was continuing, I took off my "Hello My Name Is Alice" tag and left, following Marsha's Volvo into town to find the TO OAKLAND sign. In the pitch-dark night, I considered a more immediate terror than nuclear holocaust: What if I got lost and had to wander around, mapless, among these pleasant but endless lanes? I also had the thought that, perhaps, Beyond War was the '80s equivalent of the '50s fallout shelter—something one did for the illusion of safety. But then, as I hit the freeway for the long drive home, one voice sounded clearly in my mind. It belonged to Pete. "There's nothing I can do," he had admitted during the discussion of how to avert nuclear disaster, "but I have to act like there is . . . for my kids."

Dr. Oops' Revised Sex Guide

By now everybody has read about Warner Books' recall of TV sexologist Dr. Ruth's *First Love: A Young People's Guide to Sexual Information*. The recall occurred when an alert librarian discovered a serious factual error that might, in fact, result in naive people becoming pregnant. Few, however, are aware of a similar but more monumental disaster that occurred when Dr. Oops was asleep at the word processor.

In what is shaping up as the most massive recall of a defective book in publishing history, Louis Chickenhawk, vice-president in charge of marketing for Ignoramus Books, announced that so far only sixty thousand copies of *Dr. Oops' Guide to Good Clean Sex* have been returned. Still unaccounted for are some forty thousand copies with the serial number 000-466. Citizens are advised to check their serial numbers and phone the special Ignoramus hotline immediately (1-800-BAD SEXX). Speaking at a news conference in Bayonne, New Jersey, last weekend, Chickenhawk promised purchasers their choice of a complete refund, a copy of the corrected guide, or a massage in Tijuana at no additional expense.

The Guide is the handiwork of the popular, diminutive TV commentator Dr. Ona "Oops" Von Shtuppen. Speaking with her thick Franco-Prussian accent, the sexagenarian sexologist giggled, "Well, I blew it." Flanked by her husband, a muscular thirty-seven-year-old retired gardener from Long Island (referred to by *People* magazine as "Lady Von Shtuppen's laddie"), the four-foot-seven University of Vienna graduate giggled her way through the press conference, saying she was shocked that the errors in the book were not noted earlier. "I guess I was thinking of the profits and not the pregnancies," Dr. Oops allowed with her usual candor.

At first it was believed that only one factual error regarding a woman's fertile time marred the otherwise insightful guide designed for young people preparing for the First Time (Please Be Kind). Subsequently, however, alert librarians across America have been putting their horn-rimmed noses to the page and uncovering numerous typos, bloops, and blunders that make the *Guide* a veritable child's garden of errors instead of eros. It is believed that many of these errors are the result of the author's attempt to simplify complex anatomical concepts and physiological processes. The book has been revised to include some of this complexity. Those who have not returned the book will certainly want to take note of the following errors.

1. On page 32, paragraph four: "The penis, a long shaftlike structure, consists of erectile tissue enabling it to prepare for penetration." This has been corrected in the new edition to read, "The penis, an eensy-beensy to holy-Jesus-huge-sonofagun, is an Alice in Wonderland kinda organ that can go up, down, down, up, without any regard to logic or human decency."

2. On page 75, paragraph one: "The vagina is a short vaultlike structure capable of accommodating the penis for intercourse." The corrected version reads, "The vagina-bone connected to the brain-bone, the most powerful erotic instrument in the body. The right words (and they're not *open sesame*) can improve your accommodations. Otherwise it's garbage in, garbage out."

3. On page 124, paragraph two: "Oral sex is practiced by many

people." This has been corrected to read, "Oral sex is practiced by many people although they don't talk about it."

4. On page 152, paragraph one: "For some females, it is necessary to say the Words, in order to arouse them." The corrected version reads, "Before attempting penetration, the male should pause and say, 'I love you. I want to marry you. You can have all my money. I will work for you for the rest of my life and do half the housework.' This is thought to be a powerful aphrodisiac."

5. Chapter Seven, "On Contraception: Don't Love 'Em If Ya Leave 'Em," begins with the sentence "Many people complain that using condoms is like making love in a raincoat." This has been revised to read, "Many people complain that using condoms is like making love in a Burberry."

6. Same chapter: "Many people are excited about the new contraceptive sponge that is available and carries only a very, very minor risk of toxic shock." The revision states, "Many people are excited about the new contraceptive sponge, although some have been mistakenly using Handi Wipes instead, which is of no contraceptive value and carries a significant risk of toxic schlock."

7. Same chapter: "It is possible to make love even if the diaphragm has been left in the drawer." This has been corrected to read, "It is possible to make love even if the diaphragm has been left in the drawer, providing the male ejaculates in the drawer."

8. Same chapter: Rather than bluntly asking, "Are you on the pill?" as Dr. Oops advised in the defective version, the revised *Guide* recommends that the subject be broached more tactfully. The male should stand next to the female, and without making eye-contact he should ask in an offhand manner, "So, what do you do—'ludes, uppers, downers, reds, crank, Ortho-Novum 1/50?"

9. Chapter Eight, "Sexually Transmitted Disease (STDs): Finding a Lover, Warts and All," stated, "The best way to avoid getting herpes is to insist that your partner always use a condom." This has been revised as "The best way to avoid getting herpes is to go out and gain fifty pounds."

10. Same chapter: The old version reads, "Chlamydia, now

thought to be one of the most common STDs, is often a silent infection. Women don't know they have it and pass it on." New version: "A woman should be tested for the disease and if she has it, she should greet her partner dressed as a '40s cabaret singer and begin singing, 'Tonight, my heart cries out Chlamydia . . .' "

11. The previous edition did not advise women to inspect their partners for signs of STDs. The new edition advises a complete anatomical exam. The woman should not hesitate to question any lesion she discovers. A helpful comment might be "Is that a pickle on your penis or have you got something?"

12. Men were previously told to refrain from judgment when discovering their partner had an STD. Now it is considered advisable to acknowledge the problem with a simple comment like "You filthy slut, why didn't you tell me?"

13. Page 234, paragraph three: This previously read, "Many common household objects can be used as erotic aids." To this has been appended "The blow dryer is a dangerous electronic device and has no place outside of a wash and set. Additionally, if God wanted you to use a mango, He would have given you a mango."

14. Finally, in the most well-publicized error, Dr. Oops had advised that a woman's safest time is around ovulation, the time when an egg is discharged from the ovaries. The revised version explains that, of course, this is a very dangerous time and the woman is only safe if she can prevent the man from sitting on her egg. This proves that Mother knew best when she imparted that simple piece of sexual advice: Always keep your eggs crossed.

A Plague of Pigeons,
A Scourge of Squab

The handwriting on the nursery school wall said: "Rats are here! Sign up for yours now." Surely, I wasn't the only person who reacted as if she had just seen "Malaria! Get it today."

To me, rats are what you see and say, "There goes the neighborhood." Rats are what makes you upwardly mobile. You do not want to live near them, you do not want to live with them, you do not want to sign up for them. Rats are what makes you join the rat race.

Every time my kids say they think they're "cute," I feel the kids should be sent to a wilderness survival school in The Bronx. Let 'em learn that rats is *rats*. And so are pigeons.

Nothing—even pet rats—disturbs me more than the misguided soul who has it in her heart to love pigeons. *Pigeons!* Known to any self-respecting urbanite as the "flying rat," the pigeon is currently my major foe.

To some extent, I blame my pigeon-hearted neighbor for the ongoing pigeon wars the whole area must now engage in. It was her famous last words, when the pigeons hit her eaves, that still echo in my head: "I think they're kind of cute." Surely the woman needs a few months of reconditioning in that pigeon hell-hole of Manhattan.

Last year the pigeons began roosting under our roof. We began by throwing everything we had at them—shoes, campaign buttons, a biography of Kafka. We went through the entire penny collection—about twelve dollars, not counting numismatic value —because it was the closest thing to the bed.

Finally, we hired the professionals, a group of Ph.D.-level pigeon-busters who operate under the name IPM Systems—Integrated Pest Management Systems.

"Can't you just kill them?" I asked, preferring to have my pests machine-gunned rather than managed. I learned that murder was out of the question, which is what happens when you hire non-Mafia. "It's actually illegal," the IPM man explained.

The integrated thing to do was place a bed of nails on the ledges, making a landing impossible. The neighbor tried a home-made version of this. Of course, several months later a yoga-master pigeon was cooing away on the nail bed.

Another neighbor said he experimented with a strip of carpet tacking. He claimed that a few days later the pigeon left a note saying, "This is fine. When does the rug arrive?"

Recently we all bought jet nozzles for our garden hoses and began spraying them. This works pretty well as a temporary deterrent and gives one a certain sadistic satisfaction of the if-you-can't-kill-'em-squirt-'em variety. The main problem seems to be the 6:00 A.M. wake-up cooing, which means someone must get out of bed and go downstairs to squirt them.

Ah, what inventiveness the war against nature calls forth in the human soul. Allow me to introduce the Kahn Pige-Off. Take one bathrobe. Tie sash to arm of bathrobe (for a longer reach) and lower from second-story window. Have husband tie garden hose with nozzle to robe, and then raise it to bedroom window. Next morning when the pigeons start cooing: *Blast 'em.* All this is now possible without leaving the comfort of the crib.

Soon everyone in the neighborhood will be going to bed with

their VCR remotes in one hand and their bathrobe sashes in the other.

It occurred to me that while there may be money in the Pige-Off, there are certainly other possibilities for fun and profit in pigeon-busting. Do I not live two blocks from Chez Panisse, a world-famous gourmet restaurant that serves pigeon, aka squab?

One morning, after watering the pigeons, I phoned my friend Michael Wild, chef and owner of the Bay Wolf, another famous restaurant.

"You ever serve pigeon, pal?" I asked.

"No," came the dismal reply.

"Well, what about Chez Panisse. They serve it all the time. Where do they get their pigeons from?"

"Hayward." *Hayward,* that undistinguished town. The very word was like a distant thud.

"Why Hayward?" I asked. Chez Panisse's reputation rests on the inventive use of local products. What could be more local than a neighborhood rooftop? "What's wrong with the pigeons two blocks away?"

"Those pigeons are unclean."

"Not mine," I reassured him, reaching for my hose, ". . . not mine."

Beverly Hills Anything

It started with *Beverly Hills Cop*. Then we had *Down and Out in Beverly Hills*, in which a sort of glamour became attached to picking the Garbage of the Rich and Famous.

Next, TV gave us "Beverly Hills Madam"—a glimpse at the best prostitution has to offer, a world of people so beautiful that even the madams look like Faye Dunaway—followed by a new but shortlived TV series *Leo and Liz in Beverly Hills*.

Fascination with one of the richest little neighborhoods in America seems boundless.

It's not as if there aren't other filthy-rich cities in this blessed nation. But no other community seems to have the same combination of sex, success, and celebrity; none inspires such voyeuristic fascination. And no place else plays so well on camera.

Even now, doubtless, the show biz creative departments are brainstorming bright new ideas. We'll soon be able to ogle such works of art as:

* *Beverly Hills Dental Receptionist*. This is a dramatic series that looks at the woman who helps the man who puts his hand into the mouths that eat beluga and sip Dom Pérignon. In the opener, Rhoda, the receptionist, questions Dr. Toothberg's order to have

his female patients strip to the waist before he examines their inlays. Only in Bev Hills.

* *Beverly Hills Pizza Delivery Guy* takes us along as Lorne Cavutto satisfies a voracious Angie Dickinson, who waits with bated breath for the sight of Lorne entering the gate and crossing the expansive lawn carrying a large pepperoni. Lorne, a graduate of Domino University, must dodge Mercedeses and Maseratis as he steers his Mazda down the gold-dusted corridors of Rodeo Drive.

* *Beverly Hills Bozo* features the studly yet asexual George Hamilton as George Hamilton IV, a man with everything but savoir faire. In the series opener, Hamilton gets into a brawl with the bartender at the El Padrino lounge in the Beverly Wilshire when the unfortunate lackey refuses to comply with Hamilton's request for white cabernet. "You're dead chicken," threatens Hamilton, who never eats meat.

The possibilities, you see, are infinite. Well, almost. It's hard to imagine *Beverly Hills Vice*, for example. Redundant.

And no one can do *Beverly Hills President*—that's already been done.

It's anybody's guess just how long America's lust for the glitz, the glamour, the heartbreak and the psoriasis of Beverly Hills will last. There are reasons why we just can't seem to get enough of those Bev Hills bums and bimbos.

Beverly Hills represents not just wealth but excess. It's consumerism on a binge, *indulgez-vous* to the max, Gomorrah goes Hawaiian. It's Flo Ziegfeld yelling, "More girls, more stairs, more feathers," a place that gives new meaning to the phrase "gross national product." For if, indeed, America is in an age of flaunting it, of satisfying all those pent-up demands from the low-ered-expectation Jimmy Carter era, then Beverly Hills—the concept—makes the rest of us look good.

We're all entitled now to buy a computer, a VCR, and a Caribbean vacation, but without Beverly Hills how could we live with having bought all three in the same year? Our mundane indulgences seem normal next to your pool, spa, five and a half baths, and personal exercise coach.

Any consumption guilt a new-car buyer may have felt is easily assuaged with the thought that at least it's not a Mercedes. (Those who bought a Mercedes can console themselves with "it's just a tiny one" or "it's an old one" or "at least I drive it myself.")

We're not talking materialistic puritanism here; Americans have never been reticent about owning things. But there is resentment of the overly wealthy. In order to raise one's life-style someone has to be seen as grosser than thou.

Although Beverly Hills is a bit overdone to represent the American Dream (people in Boston don't even dream about having live-in gurus), some might say that in the national mind it represents the California life-style carried to its logical conclusion —kind of Marin County plus Hollywood plus Palos Verdes Estates, all rolled up into one grotesque enchilada.

Outsiders, however, fail to understand just how different we are up here in northern California. In the north, we care. This is Beverly Hills with tears.

We march to a different script up here:

One might, for example, expect to see *Berkeley Hills Cop*, based on the story of a police officer whose penchant for pounding the heads of protesters earned him the nickname "Rambo."

Rambo has recently been forced by a Berkeley judge to seek therapy for his violent tendencies.

It's the first case of court-ordered headshrinking for head bashing.

The screenplay would show him in his recovery phase as he is taken in by a prominent leftist family and forced to serve chardonnay at their political fund-raisers.

When Rambo notes, "It's a swell joint you've got here," his hosts remind him, "Comes the revolution, everyone will live in a bay-view brown shingle."

A TV miniseries called *Nob Hill Madam* would feature a politically concerned San Francisco call girl impresario who insists that for every four-hundred-dollar trick turned, at least five bucks go to help the Nicaraguan cause.

Down and Out in Palo Alto would show what happens when a group of students decide their lives as M.B.A. candidates are meaningless.

They erect a shantytown on the Stanford campus.

One night, a homeless family from East Palo Alto moves in. Eventually parents of the students decide to stop paying their eleven-thou-a-year tuition and send the money directly to the poor family.

The students burn their yellow ties in protest.

These are shows with heart. These are stories with conscience. These are tales that prove there's more to life than palm trees and Guccis.

There are redwoods, for instance, and Reeboks.

V

*We All Need
Another Folk Hero*

The King and I

The publication of Priscilla Presley's book *Elvis and Me* and yet
another anniversary of the fall from Graceland have brought it all
back—the humiliation of having once been a fan of the man who
put white leather rhinestone capes on the map of national consciousness.

How can I explain—from a fashionably feminist perspective—
the role of Elvis in women's lives? Could I hold up my head in the
intellectual community if it were ever learned that I, like Priscilla
Beaulieu Presley, once worshiped the blue suede shoes he walked
in?

The new book will certainly draw a lot of old Elvis fans out of
the closet, and not because it debunks Elvis either. Debunking
Elvis is nothing new. Elvis is about as easy to debunk as fast food
and tract houses.

The fact that the man had a drug problem has already been
revealed. The fact that on any given day in his life he was only 10
percent there is well known. In his 1981 biography, Albert
Goldman revealed to the world that not only did the Emperor
have no clothes, he was also wearing diapers.

Lots of Decent People who always knew Elvis was scum will

be looking for the King's kinkier antics in the memoirs of his former wife. And right there on page 239 is the Ultimate Shocker. Elvis, whose gyrating pelvis sent countless mothers and fathers to the family liquor cabinet for quick sedation, insisted that Priscilla stay a virgin until their wedding night. In a world of AD/DC, Twisted Sister, and Mötley Crüe, this has got to stand out as some kind of clean joke.

Cilla, as the King called his number one, is not peddling another revisionist biography. She has written, or rather has "as told to," a reminder of the glory that was Elvis. She spent her youth living out the dream many of us cherished as we sat in our rooms with those first bulky transistor radios plastered against our ears, letting the world slip away to the tune of "I Want You, I Need You, I Love You."

Flashback to 1956. I am a tormented twelve-year-old looking for an escape from the Willie Lomanesque pathos of middle-class life. At the same time, I am possessed by biochemical demons that are coursing through my bloodstream and insisting that I can't remain a little girl. Hoping to make sense of this chaos, I turn on *The Ed Sullivan Show*, and a voice speaks right to these demons. It tells me that I am nothing but a hound dog.

Now, I have an identity. I am an Elvis fan. He is a kind of big, rockin', good ferry conducting me across the troubled waters from puberty to adolescence. I go on a popular radio show and am interviewed as an Elvis fan. I tell the DJ, "You're just jealous because Elvis has more hair on one sideburn than you have on your whole head."

I go to my first concert and stand on my chair with thousands of other girls and scream for two hours straight. I never see Elvis the whole time except for one fleeting second when I rush the police lines and ecstatically touch the trouser leg of his gold lamé suit. I discover mass hysteria is much more fun than solitary hysteria.

All over the world, boys are imitating Elvis and his moves. Every town holds a contest for the best Elvis impersonator. Boys in India who will one day come to California and design com-puters are conking up their hair. Future World Bank delegates in Brazil are turning up the collars on their pink rayon shirts. Boys who will edit *The Wall Street Journal* are standing before the mir-ror in Darien, Conn., slinging their pelvises to a zero-gravity po-sition.

The fact that grown-ups hate him is icing on the cake. My parents treat the Elvis phenomenon like a joke. My older sister, a member of the Sinatra generation, taunts me with "Where's Elvis the pelvis and his brother Enos? Haw. Haw. Haw." Other grown-ups call him indecent.

How can they call him indecent? He believes in God. He loves his mother. He buys her a pink Cadillac and a new ranch-style house. Would a bad boy do that? These are mainstream Eisen-hower-era dreams.

But my dream is to succeed in the Win a Date with Elvis con-test. I sit in my room with my *Hit Parader* magazine, studying the rules and imagining what it'll be like if I win.

Me: Love me tender, Elvis.

Him: Someday, little girl, but not now. It's a very sacred thing to me.

Me: Elvis, you're too much.

Him: No, baby, I'm just your teddy bear.

Think of it. Priscilla Presley was one of us. She won the date with Elvis, and, she insists, that's pretty much how it went, give or take a few reds and a few dexies. Her problem, of course, was that she stayed too long at the fair.

By 1958 it was all over for me. My crush on Elvis was an em-barrassment. Uncle Sam could have him. I was in high school and fielding the advances of real boys.

It wasn't just that my taste in music changed. Elvis was lower-class to the core, and I think that's what frightened parents about him. They didn't want their daughter to marry one. Other sing-ers brought black music to white people, but Elvis brought white-trash culture to the masses. He allowed middle-class girls to kill two birds with one image. They could terrify their parents and indulge in the fantasy of Lady Chatterley's rock star.

The aging of Elvis was a national nightmare. We wanted him to take diet pills rather than torment us with the idea that our fate also might include middle-age spread.

And his tacky taste mocked us. Unlike the rock stars of the '60s who used their money to marry into Society, Elvis's dreams could never make it past the lower middle class. He crowned his queen, Cilla, with a three-foot beehive hairdo.

Mick Jagger did time at the London School of Economics. Elvis didn't even have the decency to invest in southern California real estate. Instead he bought Tennessee land. Tennessee land! Mark Twain wrote an entire book, *The Gilded Age*, based on the assumption that speculating in Tennessee land was the dumbest thing around.

Then there was the matter of how he spent his time: shooting up TV sets when the shows displeased him, collecting Caddies— even the Bhagwan has the good taste to buy Rollses—and renting out amusement parks to spend his nights there riding roller coasters with his buddies. Is this any way to treat top American dollars?

As many of his old fans settled into hormonal equilibrium and draft-dodging graduate scholarship, Elvis stayed on the roller coaster of uppers and downers. His sex appeal was becoming as passé as his pompadour when, on May 1, 1967, he finally made a woman of Priscilla, his "live-in Lolita."

Nobody with any pretensions to style would have admitted liking Elvis in the '70s. He wore Vegas suits that made Sammy Davis look Amish. A 1981 B-minus movie, *Elvis and the Showgirl*, features '80s sex symbol Don Johnson as the King. Take away the salmon-colored linen jackets and put the *Miami Vice* star in those huge-collared, huge-belted leather zoot suits and we see how easily a man can commit sartorial suicide in public.

Elvis became an easy target in his last years. His once-shocking sideburns fluffed out, his voice was shot, his middle-age spread obscenely before us—he was a self-satire. A young rebel is one thing; a washed-out idol quite another.

But Priscilla Presley has come to his defense, both in her book and in her promotional interviews with Barbara Walters, the queen of investigative voyeurism. Despite the usual Baba Wawa–type questions, which amounted to "How could you do all those disgusting things with that disgusting person?" Presley remained touchingly loyal to the King. She asked us to remember the early days when he was young and lovable and too busy making the money to deal with the severe case of the social bends it caused him.

The slow decline of the King was an embarrassment to the girls who once screamed for him. And the boys who privately practiced their pelvic rock before the bathroom mirror now don pinstripes and, for wildness . . . *yellow* ties. Elvis lived out our adolescence to its logical conclusion while we went on to more mundane midlife crises.

Dethroned at home, except among the bouffant lifers, Elvis nevertheless continues to be an international symbol of greatness. When you cross the border at Tijuana, there will always be three faces immortalized in velvet: Jesus, Montezuma and Elvis Presley. The guy's in good company. He did all of us little girls proud.

Ms. Bad Manners

DEAR MS. BAD MANNERS—What is one to do with one's Jewish friends at Christmastime? That is: Does one risk offending them with a card or a gift, or is it still more offensive not to give them a card or a gift?

Of course, Ms. Bad Manners, one is not an idiot. Obviously, one does not send a Jewish friend the card with the Nativity scene on it or the one with the Holy Cross bursting through the heavens. I realize that if you're going to do it, you have to find one of those sleighride-in-the-snow scenes that say, "Happy Holidays" or a large bell that says "Season's Greetings."

But is it really necessary to search out some synagogue bazaar to find "Happy Hanukkah" cards or some appropriate gift like lox jelly or bagel ornaments? Aren't these people happy enough just to be included?

GENTILE READER—I suppose a simple "Are you religious or do I have to get *you* a present too?" won't do.

Your dilemma is worsened by the declining interest in the confrontational style in recent decades. It is a form favored by Ms. Bad Manners. Instead, we have drifted back to that repressed

Victorian mode of indirection, subtlety and innuendo, as the late Mayor Daley of Chicago so aptly put it, insinuendo.

One is not an idiot, but you may be, my dear. Your problem could be solved early in the year if you made a point of asking "these people" a simple question. Casually, while discussing investment planning or microwaving frozen broccoli, inquire: With whom would you prefer to be stranded on a desert island—Moses, Jesus, or Donahue?

If they say "Moses," you needn't buy them a damn thing. If they say "Jesus," that's an automatic fruitcake. If they say "Donahue," you must force them to join you at midnight Mass. Anyone willing to be stranded with Phil Donahue is desperately seeking spiritual guidance, and better you and your creed than some weird cult. Let's at least keep it in the Judeo-Christian family.

DEAR MS. BAD MANNERS—Happy New Year? Ha! That's a laugh. What's so happy about it?

Every year, we are forced to attend the same stupid party with the same stupid group of stupid so-called friends we have known for years. The truth is, we can't stand any of these people and their loud, drunken reveries.

The whole thing is totally predictable. Dancing and drinking for two hours. Wild kissing and fondling of other people's spouses for two hours. Puking and driving home.

In years past, we solved the problem by quietly slipping out by 11:00 P.M.—about midway through the kissing but a good hour or so before the grabbing began. In fact, we haven't had the privilege of watching anyone lose his cookies since New Year's Eve of 1980.

But this year our number's up. About a month ago, when we were with this group of friends we can't stand, someone said, "Why don't we have the party at Marge and Bill's this year?" Then they took off planning the whole thing, right down to how my husband, Bill, was going to have to dress up in a diaper and be the New Year's baby. You see what I mean? This is their idea of fun?

I'm going crazy because I don't look forward to having my house turned into a loony bin, but what can I do? I can't lie to them.

MENTAL READER—What do you mean you can't lie to them? Where would the social contract be without lies and deception?

Consider the burden. Let us suppose that every time one of the crowd invited you over, you took it upon yourself to say, "I'm not coming because I think you're a bunch of stupid idiots and if we ever get rich enough to buy new friends, we'll never set eyes on you again." Isn't a simple "We'd be delighted" ever so much easier?

Go for The Big Lie on New Year's. Let me give you permission —as they say west of Reno—to go for it. That's why you wrote to Ms. Bad Manners in the first place, isn't it? You already know how to lie, don't you? You just put your lips together and blow.

The Big Lie will depend on your serving my special Wild and Crazy Punch as soon as the guests arrive. That's: three bottles of Wild Turkey, one jigger of cola, one scoop of lime sherbet, a dash of angostura bitters (or whatever bitters you have on hand). Add ice to taste. Avoid serving high-protein snacks.

After everyone's had a glass or two, you simply set the clock ahead three hours, turn on New Year's Eve in New York, serve coffee and tofu, and kick them out.

DEAR MS. BAD MANNERS—Every year I rack my brains trying to figure out who will give me a present. Then I spend my nights lying awake thinking of the absolute best present for each person who I think will give me a present.

But inevitably disaster happens. Someone whom I hadn't thought about or who I thought hated me gives me a present, and I have nothing for them. There is no situation on earth I find more difficult than that of receiving without giving (which it is less blessed to do).

Last year a woman in my office gave me a beautiful lace handkerchief. I had nothing for her. I was so flustered that I blurted out, "But I always use Kleenex."

On the other hand, I never mind it if I have given a present to someone who doesn't give me one. Then, the burden is on them. It's their *problemo*. But I can't give gifts to everyone I know, can I?

WIMPY READER—Ms. Bad Manners is well acquainted with the sort of record keeping you're engaged in here. What's your game? Getting to heaven, or avoiding embarrassment?

For a one-way ticket to heaven you'll have to consult the travel agent of your choice. If you want to avoid embarrassment, do what Most People do. Most People have lots of gifts sitting wrapped and ready. Many of these gifts are things they themselves received last Christmas but couldn't return. (Sometimes they recognized the prewrapped specials from Payless.)

A useful technique, which really spares the time and expense of rewrapping, is to take your unopened gift down to the local hospital for X-raying. Tell them it's Halloween candy your kids forgot about.

Then when someone gives you a present, you simply grab one of similar size and say, "Here's yours. I hope you like it. I got it especially for you." A nice touch would be to quickly scrawl the recipient's name on the gift tag before handing it to him or her.

However, Ms. Bad Manners considers any additional embellishing of the story to be excessive. Comments like "I went all the way to Switzerland for it" or "I sent to L.L. Bean last spring," or "I made it myself" will not ring true when they open it and find it's a singing egg-timer from Taiwan.

Ms. Bad Manners appreciates that the holiday time is a difficult one for those susceptible to guilt. The real secret is knowing when to be blunt, when to lie, when to lie big, and when to lie low. For further guidance, I suggest my outstanding new book, *Ms. Bad Manners' Guide to Power Rudeness*.

The Saga of Honest Al

San Pablo Avenue, an old stagecoach road, runs along the western edge of Oakland like a place gentrification forgot. The flatbed trucks selling "Sweet Watermelon" look like movie props from *Song of the South*. The card rooms and saloons at the Emeryville/Oakville border have the authentic feel of the Wild West.

Here the lowliest entrepreneur, from the gambler to the street hooker to the small business person, can still make a buck.

"Honest Al" Collier is one who has come to this frontier. In another era, Al might have been one of the blacksmiths or wheelwrights whose establishments lined this road. Today, Al is part of the "automobile dismantling industry." It's not just junk anymore.

It was his business card that first attracted me to Honest Al's San Pablo Auto Wrecking Co. In addition to his name and address, the card states: "Used & New Auto Parts—Orgies Organized . . . Jury Bribes—Abortions . . . Elections Rigged . . . Wars Fought—Bars Emptied—Stud Service—Revolutions Instigated—Uprisings Quelled . . . Brain Surgery."

Was Honest Al taking that ultimate symbol of the '80s, the business card, in vain? Or is he a man who'll do anything?

Eventually I would hear Al himself dismiss the flamboyant card as "just something I saw somewhere." But to get to him I had to go through the family, who seemed eager to protect him lest the man dispel the legend. "He can talk pretty tough," one family member warned.

I am introduced to the saga of Honest Al by his wife of twenty-eight years, Minerva "Jane" Collier. ("My real name's Minerva, but everybody calls me Jane.")

"In 1963," Jane begins, "while working in a wrecking yard, a car Al was in blew up. He was burned over seventy percent of his body and spent two years in the hospital. They was afraid he'd never walk again. But as soon as he came out of the hospital—in a wheelchair—he had us wheel him down to a wrecking yard."

As Jane Collier explains it, the owner of the yard where Al was injured had promised him half his business if Al worked for him for six months and didn't sue. It is the first of many assets Al worked for and never got to appreciate. Although he put in his six months, "he never did get half the business."

As I'm speaking to Jane Collier in the little knotty-pine office at the front of the wrecking yard, her daughter Mindy, who keeps the books, and her son Flash, the counterman, come in. Later, her son James will return after high school to pull cars apart. I comment that it's rare to find a nice, old-fashioned family business like this.

"Actually, I'm divorced from Al, but we're the best of friends," she says, lighting up a Virginia Slim.

Jane Collier, an attractive woman in her early fifties with flashy blond hair and a twenty-dollar gold piece around her neck, has stood by Al since their early days in Arkansas, through junkyards in St. Louis and bars in Tennessee. After the divorce, she moved away for a while but came back because her youngest son got in trouble.

"My oldest son grew up in a wrecking yard, and we never had no problems with him. Auto wrecking has a bad name—junkyard

—but it's not that way. Every business my husband took over, he's improved."

She continues the legend of Honest Al, a country and western song of woe marked by hard work and nothing to show for it. There was a successful wrecking yard in suburban San Bruno that was sold for several hundred thou. The money was invested in a towing business that never got off the ground. "We lost all the San Bruno money."

There was another yard in Oakland that they built up and sold for $450,000. "There's a lawsuit on that now. The guy never paid us."

Nevertheless, she hopes her grandson, Michael, will follow in the family business. "Dismantling's come up in status. It's big business now. We sold that other yard for $450,000."

I feel obliged to remind her that they never got paid for it. "Yes, that's true . . ."

But Jane Collier has no regrets. She's been taken care of. She says of her husband, "He was very good. He never beat me or nothing like that."

Now she has her own little house in Oakland that she shares with her daughter and grandson. "I have an orange tree for the first time in my backyard."

She looks out the window and comments on a young lady in high heels and hot pants who's pacing in front of the shop at 9:00 A.M. "I admire a good lady who works in a hotel," she says, "but not these girls who work the corner."

Alvin Ray "Flash" Collier comes to give me a tour of the business. Flash is a twenty-six-year-old charmer with a full shock of chestnut, feathered hair culminating in a long tail that curls down his neck. He dropped out of high school to work in the wrecking business and says he has no regrets about it.

"I didn't like school," says Flash. "They don't teach nothing in high school. I was already doing something with my life, but school was interfering. I mean, school is supposed to help you with your career. I already had one."

As we walk among the stacks of hubcaps, alternators and starters, and taillights, I can't resist asking how he got the nickname. "Well, my initials were A.R.C., but they couldn't call me Arc so they called me Flash."

Oh. I ask him to explain that again, and he takes off on another elusive flight of logic having something to do with welding.

We proceed deeper into the rag-and-bone shop of the automobile. The air cleaners and flywheels and tires and doors are organized in bins marked "Chev" and "Linc" and "Olds." An airbrushed thigh of Miss May 1982 protrudes from a pile of old backseats.

When Flash reaches for a Pontiac window from the "Chev" pile, I question the organizing principles. "The inventory system is in my head," Flash explains.

We go out back to where two old employees, Joe Banks and Reverend Jones are pulling up a transmission on a forklift. There, next to a burned-out Subaru and a mangled Toronado, is a nifty looking '70 Buick Century with its rear end caved in.

"I paid $350 for it," says Flash. "The tires alone are worth $125. I'll sell the front end for $1,000. The motor's worth $500. The good door is worth $150. The glass in the bad door is worth $50 . . ." He continues counting his chickens while I wonder when they'll hatch.

Stepping into his dad's office to talk, Flash picks up his breakfast. The eggs, sausage, hash browns, and biscuits were delivered earlier from a nearby church kitchen. "It helps the community," explains Flash. Then he adds with a grin, "And for three bucks, the price is right too."

Flash has been in a wrecking yard since he could walk. When he was eight years old, he drove his first car out of the yard. "It had no body, just a motor, a trans, and two seats. I hit a diesel truck sideways and got real scared."

"I've worked five or six wrecking yards in the last ten years," he says. "When I was at a yard in Concord, they pulled me out to start a business venture in San Bruno, but they didn't hold up to their obligation. Now there's a lawsuit."

This, by now, is a familiar story, and I wondered if Flash wasn't concerned about the ups and downs of the family finances. "Look, I'm twenty-six years old and I own a business worth $300,000 right now. Three months ago, I had $300 in my pocket. I just knew the right people."

Actually, it turns out Flash is partners in the business with Honest Al, but, as he says, "We're semi-arguing. He doesn't want my old lady around." Why's that? "No good reason."

Flash explains that Honest Al, who lives in Oakland, is working in a yard in San Bruno while he, Flash, who lives in San Bruno, is working in the family business in Oakland.

"My dad is semihard to get along with. He gave me $5,000 to leave the last time we worked together. But he's been good to me. He raised me to be a successful business person. I work seven days a week." And then, as if to let me know the Bay Area in the '80s has not entirely eluded him, Flash adds, "I used to dance. I took jazzercise for five years. I've got my bag with my Reebok aerobic shoes downstairs. I'm about to join a health spa."

Before I leave that day, Flash phones his dad so I can arrange to meet him. We agree on eight the next morning. "What kind of wine do you like?" Al asks.

In the flesh the next morning, Al looks weary. "I've been a struggling businessman all my life. I come out here, make some money, go home—go back East—lose my butt, come back to California and make more money."

A tall man with graying blow-dried hair, he sits at his desk beneath two oil paintings—a reclining nude woman and a kneeling nude woman. Like his son, he wears a gold chain around his neck. Behind him is a garter labeled "I Only Sleep with the Best."

He recounts the crucial tale of his accident and what he learned from it. "I've been in pain from it every day of my life. I used to think you had to make money with your hands. This forced me to make it with my head."

He describes his business, the bucks and the lawsuits, and says, "My motto is: It's not a crime to be broke—it's a crime to stay broke."

Al speaks in mottos. "I have a temper. I can't get along with people. My motto is: I'm never wrong."

He talks about his twenty-three years as "an auto dismantler and recycler" and explains how you can tell a part is good. "I look at the condition of the interior and the motor, I smell the transmission fluid. But the truth is"—and here Honest Al grins—"I buy junk cars and sell quality used parts."

He chuckles as he describes the odd things he's found in cars. The weirdest? "One time I found a body in the backseat."

His dream, if he could ever realize it, would be "to retire to a smaller junkyard in the country, near a fishing hole. I had it one time, in Kennett County, Mo. But Sheriff Raymond Scott ran me out of town. He didn't want no brash California ass around. When he dies—I'm going to his funeral."

Seeing his family in business for themselves is another goal. He's proud of his son, Flash, and denies there's any fight. He says Flash wanted to go to college and be an architect, but "Any time he wants to, he can make $750 take-home."

Then Al gets a little red in the face as he adds, "I can take you a few miles away to Berkeley and show you kids sitting there in a stupor. Somebody forgot to tell them: There's no free lunch."

Reflecting on the ups and downs of his business, Al, who does seem genuinely honest, says, "I don't know how people live who make a couple hundred dollars a week—my employees. But you adjust . . . we're survivors. People are moving here to Oakland who appreciate what you can't get in San Francisco."

I leave Honest Al on the San Pablo Avenue frontier, reflecting on the oft-quoted words on the back of his business card:

I have worked like hell and have been worked like hell, have been drunk and got others drunk, lost all I had and now because I won't spend and lend all the little I earn and go beg, borrow or steal, I have been cussed, discussed, boycotted, talked to and talked about, lied to and lied about, hung up, robbed and damned near ruined, and the only reason I am sticking around now is to see what the hell is next!

Scooped

There's a lot of dirty stinkin' rotten stories in this dirty stinkin' rotten world—drug wars, rape, murder. That's why I'm writing about ice cream. Specifically, I'm writing about a very tiny ice-cream manufacturing plant located in an unmarked storefront in Oakland. "You call this a story?" ask the manipulated masses, a steady diet of mangled Amtrak trains, dismembered bodies, and terrorist attacks coursing through their brains. So what were you expecting? Nude photos of Jackie O?

Yes, in an innocuous-looking storefront on Grand Avenue, the Mary B. Best Extravagant Ice Cream Company is grinding out custom-made five-gallon batches of what Mary B. and her husband Jeff Best describe as "adult ice cream." "Our taste buds deteriorate with age," says Mary B. Best. "Adults need more bizazz. I make flavor intense, like very tart sorbets—"

"But," interrupts Jeff Best, "with color and texture as smooth as a sophomoric romance.

"We do get children in here occasionally," Jeff explains, "but mostly we cater to adults. We took over this site ten years ago from El Grande Ice Cream, which competed with Dreyer's, which was also up the street—hence the name Dreyer's Grand

Ice Cream. When we started, we asked ourselves: How can we make a *difference* in the field of frozen desserts?" His face, as he ponders this question, is deadly serious.

Let me interrupt here to point out that this is not just another ice-cream story. Numerous publications will purport to give you the scoop on ice cream. Generally this means an article rating ice creams as, Mary Best points out, *People* magazine did this summer. They named her Divine Decadence third best in the United States in the "exotic" category—the only San Francisco–area manufacturer so honored. Certainly I, too, could have gone around and tried Fenton's hot fudge sundaes or McCallum's butter pecan or Vivoli's Amaretto or Bott's marble fudge or Dreyer's Grand vanilla or Ortman's Swiss chocolate and called it work. But you would recognize that for what it is: a tawdry request for a handout disguised as journalism. No, I wasn't looking for a handout when I walked into the Mary B. and said, "What the hell is going on here?"

Journalistic integrity to the contrary notwithstanding, I wasn't about to turn the other cheek when, during the course of the interview, Jeff Best suddenly shoved a spoonful of Cerise Belgique in my face. Or, if he had to dip into the freezer to illustrate a point about Bavarian Strawberry—"fresh whole strawberries dipped in Marseilles chocolate, then suspended in a strawberry puree and marinated in Triple Sec before being added to an eighteen percent butter cream base"—was I about to deny him his right to gustatory visual aids? And, if I did walk out the door with a half gallon of 50-proof Crème de Menthe ice cream, could that be considered in any sense of the word *bribery* rather than, as I saw it, the logical tool of an investigative journalist?

No, I didn't go into the good shop Mary B. looking for a handout on a slow newsday. I went there because somebody told me that Jeff Best was a "character," which, to my imagination, meant a wacko, a flaming brains Alaska, a lampshade-headed prophet disguised as an ice-cream salesman. That's why I put up with being forced to eat chocolate chip ice cream right out of the batch machine while it was still soft and fluffy like whipped cream and the fresh chips of chocolate were little intense bursts of deep flavor. I was there not for the Buttered Brickle or the Apple Charlotte à la Rum or the Billy Budd Boysenberry but for the human angle, the hand that stirs the fudge that makes the Decadence. I was there to speak to Jeff and Mary because people who love people is what this writer cares about.

Jeff Best is a man in his fifties with a partial beard, graying red (tinted?) hair, a bright green jumpsuit, lots of gold jewelry, and a fake jade ring the size of a scoop of Crème de Menthe. He's not so much a wacko as a wacky, enthusiastic businessman who studied self-promotion at the Bill Shakespeare Wild West Traveling Playhouse school of acting. When Hollywood calls for the script rights to the Mary B. story, I'll ask that John Carradine be recalled to life to play Jeff Best.

Jeff is such an intense man that he frequently punctuates his comments by slapping my arm. Maybe it's being around ice cream all day that puts him in such a good mood, or maybe he's been nipping at the flavorings. "No, we don't get many children in here," he says, "but we did have one in last week. He was about to go for the Kahlua ice cream, and I explained to the mother that we used the liqueur for flavoring. I thought maybe she wouldn't want him to have any. Then she says"—and here Jeff Best throws in a shocking amount of limp wrist—"she says, 'Oh, let the little son of a bitch have some. It'll be good for him.' "

"Our mix is all natural," says Mary Best. "Milk, sugar, Cooke's vanilla, roasted nuts, but we do use ingredients such as crushed Oreo cookies in the Cookies 'n' Cream. I'm not about to call Oreo cookies a natural food." Mary Best is a large woman who, through est and various other human potential programs, has come to accept her size. On her counter is a copy of Marcia Millman's wonderful study of the world of fat people, *Such a Pretty Face.* I admire Mary for the peace she has made with the such-a-cute-little-ass culture around her. "I think people should be tarred and feathered for removing nutrients from food," she adds, "but ice cream is not a diet food. I would consider it a sin to make a low-cal ice cream. A woman came in here the other day and said, 'I really shouldn't be in here.' 'Then, out you go,' I said."

The Bests see themselves as pioneers in the growing adult gourmet ice-cream market. Unlike the Safeway supermarket across the street (and Mary points out that Safeway is the largest ice-cream manufacturer in the world), they eschew imitation flavorings, pecan-flavored peanuts, soy extenders, and other cost-saving ingredients used in Safeway's brand ice cream. The Bests' company literature fairly reeks with the buzzwords of growth groupies: "Our philosophy is simple: if we cannot create a meaningful result for a portion of the frozen dessert world, then we will not proceed . . . the Mary B. is the birthing of a new era of frozen desserts . . . we encourage your assertiveness in this wonderful world of ice cream." In short, by selling only custom-made products, the Bests offer you, the consumer, the chance to *get involved* with your ice cream.

I was taken on a grand tour of "the plant," from the poster of Einstein saying, "Great spirits have always encountered violent opposition from mediocre minds," hanging in front, to the ingredients room in back where Mary forced me to eat some fresh-made fudge for the Divine Decadence and to try the butterscotch filling that goes into her personal favorite, Butterscotch Marble. Just to be polite, I sampled some of the roasted pecans that Mary offered me as she removed them from the oven. There wasn't a food technologist in sight, but I did meet Cory, the Bests' only employee, who tends the solitary batch machine capable of producing just five gallons at a time. Then we entered the icehouse, a walk-in freezer where Mary shut the door, triggering in me the fantasy of being stuck in there for hours with her and fifty gallons of gourmet ice cream—just me, Mary, and the Chocolat du Cavalier, the Carmel Cartier, the Czar Alexandre . . .

In my wildest ice-cream fantasies I cherished the thought that, perhaps, Mary and Jeff are not just a former artist and a former hospital administrator trying to save a forty-year-old neighborhood ice creamery. Maybe they have actually been sent here from outer space to cater to my fondest adult whims—ice cream as self-expression. No doubt about it, I said, walking out to my car, where I ripped into the half gallon of Crème de Menthe with my bare hands, Mary and Jeff Best were split from a single atom and put in this world to make ice cream.

Jerry Garcia and
the Call of the Weird

He came out of suburban California twenty years ago with his latter-day beatnik, proto-hippie buddies and started playing music. And for Jerry Garcia the music's never stopped. The band was once known as the Zodiacs, then as Mother McCree's Uptown Jug Champions, then as the Warlocks. Finally it became the Grateful Dead. It's been a long, strange trip for Jerry and the boys from the bars of San Carlos and the pizza parlors of San Jose to the ballrooms of America, the concert halls of Europe, and the hearts and minds of two generations of devoted fans. Garcia remains a cult figure within a subculture.

This subculture is most apparent at a Grateful Dead concert. It may be the 1980s out there, where troops of entrepreneur-worshiping young Reaganites eat to win, dress for success, jazzercise for life, and work hard for the money. But inside of the Grateful Dead's New Year's Eve concert—an annual ritual for Deadheads —it's National Hippie Preservation Park.

The adoring sea of tie-dyed, Day-Glo Deadheads distinguishes the band's concerts from just another rock 'n' roll show. Remarkably, Dead concerts sell out without any advertising: the Deadheads find the band through organized phone trees. This

year I was included. In the great tradition of "the first one's free,"
I was contacted by a Deadhead and treated to my first night of the
living Dead.

Outside the concert, hundreds were walking around, vying for
the twelve-dollar tickets, some offering ten times that amount,
some promising things they did not have. Others held up signs
reading I NEED A MIRACLE—Deadhead code for "I want a free
ticket." Two girls came down the street outside the theater, doing
a Tweedledee-Tweedledum dance and chanting:

"One ticket is all we need.

"Trade you a ticket for a bag of weed."

Estimates of the number of Deadheads vary. Dennis McNally,
the Dead's publicist, places it at somewhere between 20,000 and
250,000. The lower number refers to the hardcore Deadheads
who follow the band on tours, traveling until their money runs
out. The higher number indicates the usual album sales and the
fans who attend at least one concert a year.

Another take on the number of Deadheads comes from Eileen
Law, the liaison between the Grateful Dead organization and the
Deadheads. In an interview with *The Golden Road*, a Bay Area
quarterly exclusively for Deadheads, Law said that the official
Deadhead mailing list (now computerized for efficiency) contains
90,000 names—up from 10,000 in 1972. Proudly, Law adds that
she carefully guards these names from exploitation, having refused requests this year from both the Mondale and the Hart
campaigns for access. Law also maintains the phones in the organization's San Rafael (Marin County) office. This phone hotline is
generally the only way Grateful Dead concerts are publicized.
Devoted Deadheads phone in weekly for news of ticket sales.
Most concerts sell out quickly. Last Halloween, a six-day run in
Berkeley sold out completely within forty-eight hours of being
announced on the hotline.

The Grateful Dead are an anomaly in the world of rock 'n' roll
because they are a performing band—making most of their
money from extensive road tours rather than record sales.

Deadheads will tell you that the band can't be recorded in the studio because the mysterious flirtation between Dead and Deadheads is missing.

It is a strange mutual dependency, resulting in an improvisational style that sometimes leaves the band sounding like amateurs but at other times carries them to the kind of ecstasy more often associated with jazz performances. And some Deadheads talk about the night they heard the Dead perform "Dark Star" or "St. Stephen" the way earlier generations of music aficionados might recall hearing Caruso in *Aida*. At times, however, the multitudes screaming for songs like "Truckin" or "Casey Jones" or "Uncle John's Band" resemble nothing so much as the piano-bar drunk who relentlessly demands "Melancholy Baby."

When I attended my first Dead concert, the experience took on an extraordinary quality only when Jerry Garcia began one of his plaintive, improvised guitar solos. Through the electronic equipment I could almost hear the banjos and tambourines of a minstrel show. Was there anything more American, I thought, than this psychedelic waif, picking and singing?

The Deadhead who guided me to "my first time" was Shelley, a Ph.D. candidate in demographics. At the concert she introduced me to her friends—lawyers, doctors, an economics professor from Yale, a software genius. Other than the hippie veneer, there was really no way to characterize the Deadheads I met, including as they did military officers, clerk-typists, and gay men. They were generally of the white-middle-class persuasion and grouped at the high and low ends of the IQ scale. There were plenty of 165's in the crowd and plenty of 94's (perhaps self-induced 94's). Your 110's were probably watching Springsteen.

There were women who appeared to have oozed out of caves in the California mountains, scantily clad hippie mommas who seem to exist on nothing but Spirulina, megadose vitamins, and cocaine. One, dressed only in a tigerskin, performed a sacrificial version of the frug. During her four-hour nonstop frenzy, she would occasionally hold out her breasts as a kind of offering for the Dead.

Also in attendance were the entire United Farmers of Humboldt and Mendocino counties wearing shirts with unabashed marijuana ads like "This Bud's for You" "Sense and Sinsemilla" and "Humboldt: the Ultimate Smoke." They stood right next to their more urban brothers who wore stylish haircuts and treated the event like a hippie aerobics class, wildly bopping in place for hours, doing a revved-up pelvic tilt that would surely surprise the guys back at the office. One could almost imagine these day-job yuppies shouting "Good workout, Jerry!" Outside the concert, where many supported their Dead habit by selling skull-and-roses shirts and decals, one fellow hawked a T-shirt that showed two teddy bears dancing. It read, "Jerrycise." Another shirt on sale showed skeletons dancing and was emblazoned with the motto "Deadercize for Life."

At the concert, I was surprised to see an acquaintance, a fairly conventional woman. She told me she'd been a Deadhead for twelve years. She had attended seventy concerts, owned and played the concert tapes that are traded underground through national magazines like *Dead Relix*, and papered her house with skull-and-roses posters. Why, I wondered, would this forty-year-old mother of two teenagers, who had risen in the ranks of a major research laboratory, live a secret life as a Deadhead? "You've never worked for NASA-Ames," she replied.

Individual band members have their own constituencies. Bobby Weir, the preppie-next-door from prosperous Atherton in the purple Lacoste shirt, has a teenybopper following (although many of these boppers are women in their thirties). Other fans are drawn to the more ambitious musicologist Phil Lesh, the bass player with a classical academic background. For some, the highlight of a Dead show is the weird extensive drum duo performed by Bill Kreutzmann and Mickey Hart. The least mythologized member is relative newcomer Brent Mydland, who plays keyboard and must compete with the memory of Ron "Pigpen" Mc-

Kernan, the wild organ and harmonica player who was part of the original band and died in the '70s of liver failure. Deadheads talk about Bobby or Phil or Bill on a first-name basis. But they especially talk about Jerry.

Perhaps none of it would have come about if a young man named Jerry Garcia hadn't been kicked out of the army in 1960 and headed back home to the San Francisco peninsula. The son of a Spanish musician and an Irish-Swedish nurse, Garcia spent his childhood, after his father died, moving through the apartments and suburban tracts of the Bay Area.

Today, Garcia shares a Marin hillside home with other members of his organization. It's a perfectly ordinary suburban house, the kind of place where middle management might live. Getting a message from Garcia proved no simple task. After several canceled appointments I was told Garcia had selected me over the *Today* show for a rare interview. That's how I happen to be seated before the fire (at 10:00 P.M.) as Garcia appears in the same unceremonious way he appears onstage—he's just there. His shaggy graying hair and large, round body suggest a creature somewhere between Father Time and Big Bird's mythological friend, the Snuffleupagus. He gives off a strange mixture of warmth and remoteness.

"I'm from San Francisco," Garcia begins, "but in a larger sense I feel like a Bay Area person. We moved to the peninsula in that furious rush people had in the '50s to get the kids out of the city. At ten, I was becoming a hoodlum so my mom moved us from San Francisco to this new, ranch-style '50s house in Menlo Park, a real nice place that was just bursting out of the ground. My mom made a lot of money, and the thrust of her thinking was to get us out of the city."

Marshall Leicester, a University of California–Santa Cruz English professor, has known Garcia since junior high in Menlo Park and even played with him in an early jug band. He recalls Garcia's "great head for words and wordplay. There was a lot of wit-play between us, that old *Mad* magazine satirical outlook that was so liberating for American kids in the '50s."

"I was a reader because I was a sickly kid," Garcia recalls. "I had asthma and spent a lot of time home in bed, so I read—that was my entertainment. This separated me a lot from everyone else.

"When I moved to the suburbs, I was hungry, really hungry to know, and I had a couple teachers who were very radical—far out. They opened the world for me. Being close to Stanford turned out to be a boon because they had all these educational experiments and they used the public schools. I had the advantage of elaborate and accelerated programs.

"That period gave me a sense that there are radical possibilities and other life-styles. Teachers always responded to me because I could draw well. I was encouraged to be an artist, and my time on the peninsula nailed that down real well." Ironically, in her quest for suburban safety, Garcia's mother may have confirmed his future as someone who would belong only up on the stage or out in the streets.

His feeling of being different, however, probably dates back to age five, when his father died suddenly in a fishing accident. Garcia was sent to live with his grandparents, who raised him for the next five years. "I think that probably ruined me for everything. It made me what I am today. I mean, they were great people but they were both working and grandparently and had no stomach for discipline." A lifelong pattern of doing as he pleased was set for Garcia.

His father's death, Garcia says, "emotionally crippled me for a long time. I couldn't even stand to hear about it until I was ten or eleven. I didn't start to get over it till then maybe because of the way it affected my mother. Also, it wasn't something I was allowed to participate in. I think it was a real problem that they tried to protect me from it. That's why I was sent to live with my grandparents."

Garcia doesn't remember his father, but he recalls hearing him play. "Sounds linger and I can recall them, you know, the way some people can recall smells. I can hear a sound and all of a sudden it will transport me. I remember him breaking out the clarinet."

Garcia chooses his words thoughtfully, carefully, as he talks about his father's music. "I remember the sound of the clarinet more than the tunes—the clarinet has that lovely, woody quality, especially in the relaxed middle register. That sound is very present in my ear. I can hear that clarinet right now. I don't know what the tunes were, but I do remember Stephen Foster kind of tunes. You know, nice little melodies." I thought about "Brokedown Palace," the Dead's farewell song at concerts, a Foster-like tune with lyrics that tell of leaving one home and looking for another.

"I wish I could have a better picture of my father as a musician. He was a jazz musician, hip for his day, apparently. I remember poking around, looking at some of the arrangements his band used to play, and I thought they were pretty hip. He was a genre player like I am, an idiom player."

Garcia's first leap into his father's footsteps came in 1957 when he hocked the accordion his mother gave him for his fifteenth birthday and got an electric guitar. "When I got that guitar, a Danelectro, a good cheap pawnshop guitar—very cheap but nice and loud—I was beside myself. I was so happy to get it. I wanted to be an artist but I fell in love with rock 'n' roll—Chuck Berry, Little Richard. . . . I lean more to the rhythm and blues, the black music, because that's what I listened to first.

"Later, I listened to the crossover guys, the rockabilly guys, the white guys—Elvis Presley, Jerry Lee Lewis, Carl Perkins—those kind of guys. I loved them, too. You know, the stuff. The real stuff." He giggles. "I came right to the surface for that. Yeah. Yeah. Me. Me. That's for me!"

By seventeen, Garcia was fed up with high school and dropped out. He joined the army, hoping to see the world, to go to Germany or Japan or Korea. He was sent to Fort Winfield Scott, the majestic old structure just beneath the Golden Gate Bridge. There he saw other guys like himself, bigger "screw-ups," boys with "Live Fast, Die Young" tattoos. After almost a year of being involved in "all these soap opera scenes" and going AWOL to be with a friend who was threatening to commit suicide, Garcia was dishonorably discharged. "These things piled up and I was out. So I went to Palo Alto and hung out.

"I met Hunter there—Bob Hunter—the guy I write music with. I moved into my car. He just got out of the National Guard. He also bought this old car like I did and it broke down just like mine did and we were both living in this empty lot in East Palo Alto in these broken-down cars. So I had a pal. We were the beginning of this little community. We started going to the local coffeehouse, St. Michael's Alley, and pretty soon that became our social life. Actually, that became the ground floor for the Grateful Dead."

Garcia recalls this period in his life as "just enormous fun"— hanging out at St. Michael's Alley at night and Kepler's book-store during the day. "That was my day job: I practiced guitar and read books at Kepler's. You can think of the inside of Kepler's as the Greenwich Village part of it and the parking lot to the beach as the California Experience."

During the early '60s, Garcia began to play acoustic guitar at various South Bay clubs, forming different bands with his friends. A friend of mine, who was Garcia's girlfriend in 1961, recalls sitting with him in the front row of Joan Baez's concert at Palo Alto High that summer. He watched Baez intently, saying, "I can do that! I can beat her technique." But slowly he moved from folk songs to rock 'n' roll. He played the Tangent in Palo Alto, the Boar's Head in San Carlos and the Off Stage in San Jose. All of which, he says, "was part of the networking of what be-came the hippie world—what became the Haight-Ashbury even-tually."

Garcia and friends moved into a large house behind Stanford, not far from writer Ken Kesey's Perry Lane house where, Garcia says, "Kesey lived with older people, a college scene. We were all the young total freaks and we were into drugs heavy. Kesey's scene was a little more adult and not so drug-oriented. This is before acid. I didn't like to drink ever, and drugs were much more fun for me. I loved pot. Pot was right up my alley. Anything that makes you laugh and makes it so that you love to eat—to me, that's fun." Garcia, who does not appear to need help in the appetite department, laughs heartily. Garcia views drug use as a very personal matter, "more personal than a person's sex life." But he has also seen people like Janis Joplin and Pigpen die of drug- and alcohol-related problems, and says, "it's not for everyone."

A sobering moment occurred in 1961 when he was in an automobile accident that killed a friend, Paul Speegle. The incident is part of Grateful Dead lore: some claim the group's name comes from this accident because Garcia supposedly traded places with Speegle in the car right before the crash. "Something like that happened," he recalls, "but that wasn't the important part for me. At that time I wasn't going anywhere. I was playing acoustic guitar and thinking of myself as an artist but not going to art school. This accident put some focus, some intensity and desire, into our life. It's like somebody important was gone from our little scene, someone who had real talent and who might have been great—it was necessary now to fill in, to take up the slack. Three of us survived and we were all profoundly affected."

Eventually, Garcia, Weir, Kreutzmann, Lesh, and Pigpen would form the Warlocks. One night Ken Kesey, who had discovered LSD as a volunteer in a Menlo Park Veterans Administration hospital experiment, invited them to play at a strange party. "The first Acid Test was in San Jose," Garcia recalls. "We were freshly unemployed, burned out on bar gigs, so we brought all our gear down there. We set up our snazzy rock 'n' roll stuff on one side of the room and Kesey and the Pranksters had all their funky weird stuff on the other side of the living room. We cranked up, went completely hog bananas wild and then we packed up and went home. We had this tremendous purpose—a completely organized rock 'n' roll band in the middle of their formless party." The Warlocks took their new acid-rock sound to Magoo's, a pizza parlor in Menlo Park. "There was pandemonium that very first show and it really hasn't changed much. It was like one of those old rock 'n' roll movies from the '50s."

If it hasn't changed much, is it going anywhere? How is Jerry Garcia fitting into Reagan's America? "Very poorly," Garcia says. "I've often had the horrible suspicion that those of us who are out here on this fringe going 'Huuuuuuuhhhh' are creating the Moral Majority over there going 'Huuuuuuhhhhh.' I know there must be some connection because we represent the poles and the pendulum swings between. But I just don't like that guy Reagan. I didn't like his movies and I don't like his politics. I like things wide open, with question marks hanging over it, everything changing—nothing settled.

"I've never been that uncomfortable with the world. I've always had my stuff to do and that always seemed more important to me than paying attention to what the world was doing. I feel part of a small, tight, long-lived community that is similarly purposeful. I don't see us formed that much by the world or contributing dissidence to it. We're not that important. We could drop out and they wouldn't miss us, or they could drop out and we wouldn't miss them. It's just too bad we all have to live on the same planet."

Garcia is currently at work on a script for a movie about outer space. He says he belongs with those who heed "the call of the weird." So space is the place, I think, where Jerry Garcia will finally be at home.

Professor of Gambling

Odds are you haven't heard of Mike Orkin's class in gambling. And if you saw him walking down the street you'd peg him as a long shot for the lead in the movie *The Nutty Professor*. In his black T-shirt with biceps bulging and with his highway-patrolman-turned-murderer sunglasses, Dr. Orkin looks more like a casino enforcer than head of a university statistics department.

Orkin teaches Statistics 2088—"the only college course in the United States that is entirely devoted to games of chance"—in the decidedly unexperimental atmosphere of the California State University at Hayward. More remarkable to those who fall into the "math spaz" category is that Stat 2088, which requires no mathematics or statistics background, will satisfy the university's only math requirement. Now you can pick up the old B.S. and a few pointers on your way to Fat City.

Not quite, says the good professor, who claims his motivation for teaching the class was to attract more majors to statistics. "I noticed that when I was teaching statistics to other majors the most excitement occurred when I talked about games of chance." Plus, he insists, he is just a socially responsible kind of guy. "I feel I'm doing a social service to discourage people from becoming gamblers—not by moral arguments but by mathematical arguments."

Lee (Lee the Flea) Barry, a cupcake baker by night and an Orkin student by day, says the class did not discourage him from gambling. He feels Orkin understands that games of chance are a form of entertainment. "I've lost three or four or five hundred dollars, but everybody needs a little play money to have a good time with. My friends and I like to say that when we get to the top of that path into Nevada, our money turns into bananas."

At a recent class, Orkin seemed bent on proving that the citizens of California are not playing with a full deck. In the fourth week of the session, Orkin was discussing the California lottery, using probability theory to demonstrate that the expected win on a given ticket is minus fifty-four cents. In previous weeks he'd done a similar number on casino games, and he'll prove the suckerability quotient on horse racing in the weeks ahead.

Before I entered Orkin's class in the science building, I found myself drawn to the cafeteria at Cal State, a school I attended in the early '70s when I was adding to my baccalaureate collection. I noticed some changes had occurred in the past decade. The formerly aseptic cafeteria was now "La Cocina" and featured a display of baguettes, a salad bar, and a white-domed chef slicing beef. "But it's the same beef as fifteen years ago," said Orkin, in a different formulation of the suckerability quotient.

The campus still has a solid, no-nonsense, lower-middle-class feel, but the hottest spot during the noon hour is not The Puzzle —a new beer joint—it's the game room, where throngs of young men with hair moussed up to heaven are shooting pool or trying their luck at games like Defender, Spy Hunter, and Rush 'n Attack.

Meanwhile, the students of gambling are gathering around one-time judo black belt Dr. Orkin, who is stomping their dreams. "Playing the California lottery may be more convenient than driving to Lake Tahoe, but in terms of cold, hard mathematical facts, it's worse than any game in Nevada."

Orkin has just proved that for the lottery game, the house (i.e., the State of California) has a 54 percent advantage compared to a 5.3 percent casino advantage in roulette or a 1.4 percent casino advantage in craps. Only keno, where the house has a 25 percent advantage, comes anywhere near the lottery as a sucker's game. However, Orkin allows that keno "requires the least consciousness . . . you can actually be comatose and play."

His class is held in one of those long, dingy, windowless rooms with a periodic table for art, fluorescent lights for atmosphere, and a low-level hum in the background.

Only one or two of the students (who are typically young, male, and mustachioed) are nodding off. Most are participating with stories about friends who won but lost, questions about strategies, and speculation on the social good of the lottery. Orkin deflates the it-helps-the-schools argument by pointing out that only 38 percent of the money collected goes to the schools. The rest goes to administer and advertise the lottery and finance the payoffs.

Later, when I visit Orkin at his home, a typical Berkeley home (complete with a cat throwing up on the hardwood floor), he is even more scathing in his attack on the lottery. "It's taxation of the poor. Studies show the lotteries attract a disproportionate number of low-income people. Since poor people can't invest in real estate or play the stock market, they're forced to play the bad games—Reno, the track, and the lottery."

Oddly enough, Stat 2088 was not all that much more fun than other math classes. You still need to add higher numbers than you have fingers. You still need to take tests. Although the jargon of this world—phrases like "payoff matrix" and "tit-for-tat strategies"—is a bit more colorful, you still need to do work. "I was raised on the Jewish work ethic," says Orkin, who says that except for the odd game of blackjack, he never gambles.

Orkin is a lifelong student of chance. "It's randomness—in life, in the I Ching and in casino games—which has always been my interest." He explains that probability theory, the science of chance, began when a seventeenth-century French nobleman hired the famed mathematician Pascal to improve the odds in his favorite dice game. "Pascal was the first mathematical consultant."

Another major mathematical application to gambling occurred in the early 1960s when Ed Thorp, a University of California–Irvine mathematician and author of *Beat the Dealer*, developed a computer simulation for blackjack.

I wondered when Orkin was going to cash in his chips and start consulting for the casinos.

If Orkin isn't heeding the call of the buck himself, he certainly hears its siren song all around him. "You go skiing—you see the casinos. You pick up the sports section, you get the betting lines. You walk into the 7-Eleven, and there's the lottery. Gambling fits into an instant-action, speeded-up world. Everybody from the president on down is looking at short-term results."

But, I ask him, isn't the gambling explosion happening because so many people are making money these days? Young entrepreneurs have replaced rock stars as the new heroes. *Inc. Magazine* is the *Rolling Stone* for the '80s. Isn't gambling the only way a poor person can buy a ticket to dream of entering the wonderful world of limos, designer clothes, and designer drugs?

"Except," says Orkin, "people have a misconception. They think if you start out with a bad game you can escape it with a strategy, but the mathematical fact is that given an unfair game, there's no strategy to turn it into a good one."

It's the considered opinion of this professor of gambling that all the games of chance he studies are "bad" from a mathematical point of view. How, then, does he explain the attraction of gambling to intelligent, even noncompulsive players?

He describes a party he attended when a friend of his, "the dean of a law school," won fifteen grand on a two-buck Pick Six ticket at the racetrack. At the celebration he met a psychiatrist who analyzed his love of the track. "He used some psychiatric term—*framing*, I think it was—and said his greatest pleasure was in framing his horse at the winning moment. He said the experience of watching his horse cross the finish line was the most exciting emotional experience he knew, more exciting even than sex."

As Orkin said this I realized why I had headed straight for the Cal State cafeteria when I arrived on the campus. I recalled a day fifteen years ago when I was eating my lunch and, out of the blue, the man in charge of financial aid called me over to his table. "Come by my office," he said, "we've got an extra three hundred for you." I remember exactly where I was sitting when he called me over and what I was wearing—the purple T-shirt, the one I kept until it had too many holes to wear.

The T-shirt was lucky. The cafeteria was lucky too. No doubt about it, I framed that moment.

The smart money would have Mike Orkin applying math to gambling, but instead he applies gambling to math. He hopes to use the excitement of trying to beat the odds, the inherent sexiness of getting something for nothing, to teach students complex mathematical ideas.

"Things are going to get interesting next week when we start playing blackjack in class," he said. "Then I'm going to have my friend Les, the racing fanatic, come in and predict a horse race minutes before we listen to it on the radio."

Where was this guy when I was flunking math for nonmajors?

She Saved
the Lounging Suit

In an otherwise nondescript drawer in a carefully secured room deep in the Oakland Museum, an historic lounging suit lies untouched by human hands.

The suit, from Nancy Reagan's personal wardrobe, is one of a number of garments donated by the First Lady in 1982 to museums across the country. It has, happily, escaped the deterioration that has made Mrs. Reagan's Inaugural gown a cause for national concern.

While Mrs. Reagan's Galanos gown is sinking in the Smithsonian, her silk Adolfo outfit rests in two perfect pieces in the Oakland Museum's history department. Inez Brooks-Meyers, curator of costumes and textiles, is quick to assure this writer that the Oakland Museum is not giving the Reagan garments the royal hanger. "We treat all the garments specially," she insists.

Like many other valued items in the Oakland collection, the lounging outfit is preserved in "horizontal" storage. That is, it is lying down horizontally in a special enclosed rack for textiles. According to Brooks-Meyers, "the shelf moves in and out so that you don't have to touch it."

Emphasizing the hazards of vertical storage, she adds, "The top of the tunic is pleated, so we didn't want to put it on a hanger. Then gravity would take its toll."

To further preserve this historic leisurewear, it is covered with muslin and the two pieces are protected by acid-free tissue, a special paper designed for museum storage that protects garments from the ravages of "acid which attacks the fiber."

Brooks-Meyers speaks with quiet authority as she explains how much other museums—those fortunate enough to receive donations from Mrs. Reagan—have learned from the tragic situation at the Smithsonian, where gowns on display are rapidly deteriorating.

Although much of the nation was first alerted to the situation by cartoonist Garry Trudeau, and assumed it was a joke, preserving Mrs. Reagan's rags is no laughing matter. "It's very difficult to maintain garments when they are on constant exhibit," says Brooks-Meyers. Of the Smithsonian gown, the cause of national concern, she comments: "I'm surprised that Mrs. Reagan's gown has suffered so quickly, but gravity really pulls on beaded things. That garment, being beaded, is subject to a gravity pull."

One reason the lounging outfit in Oakland has not suffered gravity's pull or acid's reign is because it has never been displayed. Although Brooks-Meyers told San Francisco *Chronicle* columnist Herb Caen in 1982 that the treasure would go on display "soon," it is still in horizontal storage. This is because the Oakland Museum displays garments along with other artifacts as part of larger social themes. Apparently the museum has yet to do a comprehensive show on lounging.

"We try to relate the costume to some aspect of social history and significant individuals. Of course, Mrs. Reagan having been a First Lady here in California and then in Washington is special; but an exhibit does not consist of one garment."

She explains that the Reagan outfit is one of many historic items the museum has in its high-tech mothballs. "We have a shirt from Governor Earl Warren that he wore when he was governor —not chief justice. We've got a fan from the Haas-Lilienthal family—of course, they own Levi Strauss. And we have items from Mrs. Isaac Requa—her husband was involved in the Comstock Lode, and they were a prominent late-nineteenth-century Piedmont family. Their house was The Highlands, which became an important name in Piedmont. That's the name of the high school football team—the Highlanders."

This is Brooks-Meyers's way of saying that the lounging outfit is no more special to the Oakland Museum than any other treasure. When asked what she thought the black silk trousers and the yellow pleated top with black floral print might be worth off the rack or out of horizontal storage, she refused to speculate. "We don't discuss the value of any garment."

A spokeswoman for Adolfo said that replacing the outfit today would cost between $1,850 and $2,200. She quickly added, "But I wouldn't make it anymore."

Brooks-Meyers does have some ideas for future exhibit themes that could include the Reagan outfit, but she refused to let on what those might be.

Meanwhile, the only way to see the lounging suit is through a written request to the museum. Curiosity seekers need not apply.

Only those involved in "historic research" will be considered. Not, Brooks-Meyers explains, "because we're trying to be snooty. We just don't have that many people to deal with it. We have other responsibilities."

Textile preservation is only a small portion of the limited budget of the history department of the Oakland Museum, which is financed by city taxes. Unless a major private effort is undertaken here, there are no immediate plans to enable the idle and curious to view Mrs. Reagan's gift to Oakland.

In addition to budgetary and thematic concerns, Inez Brooks-Meyers must weigh the risks of displaying historic artifacts. "Obviously, by putting the things out, their doom is sealed."

So while everything else in the San Francisco Bay Area is coming out of the closet, the lounging outfit stays.

VI

My Life as a Gal

Back-to-Schools

In this year of Our Lord, the hottest item of clothing a girl can own is a pair of Guess jeans. Somehow this Paris-based manufacturer has convinced the children of the material world that their rugged, tight-ankled denim is a necessity of life. At fifty bucks a pair the quest for Guess really puts one's parental love on the line. Our message to our daughter: Clothes aren't everything—especially at those prices. Her message to us: Everybody's got Guess jeans. The culture's message: Don't go back to school without them.

This year, the adolescent girl clothing market is expected to reach $8 billion. Although our daughter is not quite a teenager, she seems to be in the avant-garde of desire. Telling her these things are unimportant works no better for her than it once did for us. Our dilemma as parents: how to give our child what she wants and still not feel like total suckers.

When we planned a trip down to southern California, my daughter piped up that she heard there was a Guess outlet somewhere in Los Angeles. I won't say we went to L.A. looking for bargain jeans, but the hunt gave our trip some focus. In fact, it was in pursuit of this goal that we ended up in the middle of a native Angeleno ritual, the truly bizarre bazaar of the L.A. garment district, a study in postindustrial primitivism. Being in the decaying brick heart of a city, among various ethnic groups speaking in many strange tongues, was an experience unlike any I've had in California. It took me back—back in time, "back East," as the Californians say.

Although it is a major retailing event ("the Christmas of the children's clothing industry," according to the chairman of Toys Я Us) the ritual of back-to-school also has a folkloric quality. It is a time for starting anew, for playing roles, for considering possibilities. When I thought back to all the first days of school I went through for nearly twenty-five years, when I backtracked through all the halls of ivy, the groves of academe, the colleges of hard knocks that left their mark on my transcripts and psyche, I found I was taking my daughter's quest for Guess seriously.

It was on a sunny September morning toward the end of 1949 that I first participated in the great American ritual of back-to-school. I was a first-generation American. To enter the portals of education was to throw my raffle ticket into the American Dream hopper. Anything was possible.

My parents both came from large Eastern European immigrant families and were both orthodox members of a book-worshiping religion. Neither of them were able to continue school beyond the tenth grade because they had to go to work to help support their families.

My parents were eager to go modern, to shed all traces of their greenhorn past. As a result I would walk about a mile to attend a public school rather than the one-room yeshiva across the street. Public schools were a sign of hipness to my parents, and I was grateful. In these booming postwar years, the dark-garbed yeshiva kids looked to me like some plain Amish sect.

My first back-to-school day began early in the morning. My mother scrubbed me until all microscopic traces of dirt were gone. Then she pulled my hair into two braids and finished each pigtail with a yellow silk bow. Clothes, the first trappings of upward mobility, were terribly important to my mother. I can still hear her breathing, panting, as she took out the new yellow dress she had bought me a month before for the First Day. The finishing touch was a lacy white pinafore that went over the dress. I was Alice—about to go down the rabbit hole of lower education.

At the doors of Chicago's John Milton Gregory School, 3715 West Polk Street, I let go of my mother's hand. Before the day was over, I would learn how to make a snake out of clay, a chain out of paper strips, and a sheriff's badge out of the cap to my milk bottle, and I would learn to sing "America the Beautiful." I had never seen the purple mountains, the spacious skies, or the amber waves of grain, but I trusted they were out there somewhere.

That morning, as I stood on the steps about to enter the monumental building, my heart was pounding with anxiety. Would I make the grade? Would I be a credit to my race? Would I be the student the Jewish People demanded? As these thoughts raced through my head, something flew over me. Later, I would see it as an omen, a harbinger, an instrument of the Evil Eye, there to tell me that life held something other than success or failure for me. A strange, marked path was to be mine. As I walked into the door, a pigeon went splat all over my new white pinafore.

When we got to L.A., we called the Guess Company and got the name of a shop in something called "the Cooper Building" where, we were told, Guess products were sold at discount. I phoned ahead and a man with a thick accent said, "Yeah, we got. You come in later. I unpack now—five hundred items."

"Of course, the Cooper Building," said Cousin Laura, who grew up in Beverly Hills, "I've been going there as long as I can remember." Laura, like a lot of people I know, was the relatively poor kid in a rich town but, as she explained, everyone in L.A. shops the garment district before the start of school. In the City of Angels, where shopping is a way of life, wholesale is a matter of pride.

When we arrived at the blocks of old buildings and outdoor markets known as the garment district, the streets were already swarming with mobs of mothers and daughters in the process of committing a back-to-school consumer coup. It was like a grammar school pageant, Chicago's Maxwell Street, and New York's Lower East Side all rolled into one. ("You should have seen the garment district when I was growing up," said Cousin Laura. "Then, you'd have to walk through the sweatshops and actually see the garments being sewn. Now, instead of bringing workers across the border, they just bring the finished garments. . . .") There were mothers and daughters from Iran, from Israel, from Mexico, from Vietnam, from Russia, from Ethiopia, from Holmby Hills, from San Clemente, from Torrance, and probably even some who had started in Chicago. All were there looking for the right stuff for opening day, the costume that said who they were, who they wanted to be.

By the time I graduated from grammar school, the school had changed considerably and so had I (if the word *changed* even touches on the process of puberty). By the eighth grade the little silver stars in my report card had been replaced by red marks in "conforms to school regulations, accepts responsibility, and keeps profitably busy."

After graduation, my parents moved across town to a New Jerusalem called Rogers Park. The streets were clean, the houses new structures of blond brick with skinny stone fireplaces like in *I Love Lucy,* and the kids not only had their own rooms but their own cars, their own phones, their own phonographs, and their own knotty-pine recreation rooms with Ping-Pong tables. My first day of high school, I looked up before I entered the pillars of the massive Roman Revival building, not knowing a soul in the school of five thousand kids.

I hated the new neighborhood. I thought the boys in Bermudas looked "fruity" and the girls with their ponytails and little collegiate pleated skirts were all snobs. I wore a black skirt so tight that I needed a girdle to slide into it and a turquoise blue sweater that I thought made me look like Gina Lollobrigida's twin sister. My pink babushka, which had the words *You ain't nothin' but a hound dog* on it, I knotted right *on* my chin, not under it, in the manner of the "hoody" girls I had left across the tracks.

I got in trouble the first day. In Spanish class the teacher got mad at me when she caught me putting on makeup during class. "Would you like to come up here and do that, *señorita?*" she asked. I sauntered to the front of the class smirking, took out my compact, and globbed on still more dark red lipstick.

Lunch was a real dilemma. There were four nearby stores as well as the school lunchroom. I went to a store called Es and Gertie's for my hot dog, fries, and Coke. I quickly learned this was a big mistake. A boy from my social studies class explained the system: The lunchroom was for jerks and "grade sucks"; Harry's was for the popular Jewish kids; Bob's was for the popular gentile kids; the Ridge House was for unpopular kids of all backgrounds; and Es and Gertie's was strictly for sluts and juvenile delinquents. Just eating at Es and Gertie's *once* probably gave me a bad rep. To go there twice, my informant told me, would label me a "skank" the rest of my life.

That could have been my last first-day-of-school, but it wasn't. There were many more to come. Four years later I was Betty Coed going off to a midwestern Big Ten school. I bought my outfits from the College Shop. There, girls dressed in the latest styles—shetland sweaters and plaid slacks—sold similar items under banners that said "Harvard, Princeton, and Yale," colleges not yet contaminated by women.

At that time the University of Illinois had curfew hours for women, and we were not allowed to live in apartments or rooming houses. We had a choice between massive dormitories that looked like cell blocks in some Ida Lupino women's prison movie —or sororities. I was particularly terrified of the legendary green gravy dinners in the dorms, and following my best friend, Penny, I went through sorority rush. There were two black sororities, five Jewish sororities, and thirty white gentile sororities. This was not California in the '80s. We didn't blend in. Although I would only be considered for my ethnic group, I was forced to go through the charade of talking to endless Mary Lous and Sally Janes at Phi Shiksa Shiksa.

One of the Jewish houses served fruit salad in a watermelon shell carved like a basket and chopped liver molded like a pineapple. That was the one for me. When Penny said she was joining that house, I followed her and joined Phi Sigma Sigma (or "Phi Piggie Piggie," as we were known on campus). A year later Penny flunked out and I was left holding the chopped liver and living with some of the most vapid people I have ever known. *Animal House* didn't do the scene justice. The amount of money these women spent on lingerie would be enough to feed an entire village in Africa for the rest of history.

When I remembered what wearing the wrong skirt or tying a scarf the wrong way could mean back in school, I knew why I was there in the smoggiest and most congested part of L.A. supporting my child in the obsessive search for the right jeans.

"Not unpack yet," said the owner of the shop, a man wearing four gold chains including one with a gold bar that said "fourteen karat." "You come back."

"But we're only in town one day," I implored.

He threw up his hands: "I do my best."

It was tempting to tell my daughter that "clothes don't really matter, the person does," or that "most of the world's peoples are looking for food, not designer clothes," or a number of other things that would mean about as much to her as when my mother used to say, "If we'd stayed in Europe, we'd be dead."

Not everything was grim at the Old University of Illinois. I began to hang around with my professors, foreign students, and the hip black students in the dorm canteen (although the sorority had a rule prohibiting its members from "twisting in the canteen"). Along the way I also met the not-so-sartorially-correct bohos and misfits who would take me on that long and winding road that inevitably leads to Berkeley. My life began to revolve around my career plan rather than my wardrobe: I was to be a poet. This required that you spend a lot of time talking to other people who sat in public places writing in little notebooks.

In my junior year of college, I moved to New York to study poetry at the only school in the country that had no rules for women and no football team—the Columbia University School of General Studies. It was obvious that first day that I had plunged myself into the Grand Canyon of alienation, the Upper West Side of New York. Not only did I spend months without anyone speaking a civil word to me, but the school itself turned out to be a real loony bin of people who had been having nervous breakdowns at Princeton and Radcliffe. I remember one day, in the middle of Late Victorian Poets, a woman stood up in the back of the class and, for no apparent reason, started screaming, "I can't stand it anymore." As she stood there sobbing the kindly professor asked to no avail, "Was it something I said? Something Tennyson said? Morris? One of the Rossettis?"

At Columbia I learned to wear all the correct attitudes of the time toward Western Civ. Jane Austen was hot. Shelley was not. C. P. Snow was a schnook. F. R. Leavis was cool, etc. etc. Also at Columbia, I had my first introduction to the Left, not just from my boyfriends, who were all second-generation Brooklyn socialists, but from the people in my building who were involved in revolutions throughout the world. One day I picked up the New York *Daily News* and saw a photo of the Haitians who had lived across the hall—beheaded by Papa Doc.

I tried, while at Columbia, to take a famous course in the novel that Lionel Trilling was teaching. I was told by a dean that the presence of a woman "would destroy the pristineness of the class." I swear on a stack of Thackerays, he really said that.

I moved to San Francisco after college graduation and went back to school at San Francisco State College. It was a real oasis after the formality and pomposity of Columbia University. I was called by my first name. Men didn't wear ties and women didn't wear heels. A wild girl named Jane Dornacker, who ran around barefoot and was known as Jane the Earthmother, was crowned homecoming queen that fall.

I took a sociology class and we sat around eating some kind of mushroom and writing a report on "Emerging Bohemian Subcultures in the Haight-Ashbury District." Within a month, I got out of poetry. In one of the great upwardly mobile career decisions of my life, I decided to become a high school teacher. In the fall of 1966 I went back to school on the other side of the desk.

By 1969, my teaching career was over, the victim of a rightwing inspired purge at the school where I taught. But I didn't care, I was twenty-five. I had my retirement check for a thousand dollars signed by State Controller Houston P. Flournoy. And for the first time in my life, I didn't start school when school started. Instead, on those September morns, free as a bird, I'd walk up to the bus stops at 7:00 A.M. and watch the commuters leave as I sang, "I love you Houston P. Flournoy . . ." When I did sign up for classes, it was at the Free U, where I studied Introductory Astrology, Essentials of Batik, and Breadmaking 101. I needn't worry about back-to-school clothes. I could always find them in the Free Box or—whatever.

I was such a lifer that two years after I vowed that I was through with schools, that I would just work in a factory or be a waitress if I had to, I was back in the slammer. But what an incredible place I went back-to-school to that time. It was called Merritt College and later Grove Street College, a crumbling old Julia Morgan–style building surrounded by temporary huts in Oakland near the Berkeley border. The place was already legendary as the site where Huey Newton and Bobby Seale met and founded the Black Panther Party. For me it was a place where I could finally learn and have a good time. I went there to learn science—an area I had abandoned when I consciously decided to become a Bad Girl in the eighth grade.

Grove Street College was like an old Mickey Rooney movie: Hey kids, let's put on a school in a barn. While we heard stories of competitive Cal students stealing each other's chemistry lab notes, we worked collaboratively in the best tradition of science. Oddly enough, thinking about Avogadro's Number did wonders for my poetry.

Our teachers were especially patient with the women students like myself who were terrorized by such exacting concepts as numbers. Nearly half the women I knew in the Berkeley Women's Health Collective went on to become doctors or nurses after their science headstart program at Grove Street. It was the most exciting time of my life, intellectually, since the fifth grade. What a shock, then, when I went back to school in the fall of 1971, to find armed Oakland police moving our laboratory equipment up to the new Merritt campus in the Oakland hills. I spent that fall back at school on the picket line, dressed in U.S. Army surplus, and screaming at the Oakland police.

"Sorry, not unpack yet. You come back," said the man with the gold chains. Our time and patience were running out. The freeways of L.A. were waiting to treat us to the Indy 500 of rush hours. Our youngest child, sixty pounds of fun, was demanding to be carried. When we figured in the hourly wage of two adults, the cost of discount jeans was going up. Of course, there was more to the experience than money.

Finally the man with the chains took pity on us and said, "Okay, you come with me." He took us into the Back Room—the absolute inner sanctum of the discount universe, and there were two pairs of the sacred cloth in my daughter's size. We grabbed them like bone-dry bikers spotting a Coke machine in the Sierra. Fifty dollars for two pairs. What a bargain. We thanked the man repeatedly for the opportunity. He was all smiles. He, too, understood the thrill of the hunt, the ecstasy of let's make a deal.

I thought I was finally through with the cultural ritual of back-to-school. No more teachers. No more books. However, having children, I've discovered, forces you to relive these rites of passage from a different vantage point. As a parent, back-to-school takes on a new meaning. On the one hand, it's a time when life returns to normal, when the unpredictable rhythms of summer fade, when I can count on having the house to myself for a few hours. I've now seen two girls through the terror of the first day of kindergarten. The terror was mine. Both times, I hid in the bushes at recess like some pervert to make sure they were okay.

On the other hand, with one girl on the brink of adolescence, the ritual has turned costly. I am suddenly expected to contribute my share to that $8 billion market. In an effort to argue our daughter out of extravagance, to abuse her with logic, my husband calculated the average contribution. We discovered, to our horror, that this comes to nearly $500 per girl each September. We concealed this fact from our daughter.

When I backtrack through the back-to-school days of my life, I realize how different from the dreams of my parents, the hopes of my People, the insomniac fantasies I had the nights before school started, the events that actually transpired were. Still, it is a time when anything *is* possible, a time to play roles, a time to dress up. When the portals of learning open this year, there are going to be a lot of Guess jeans and a lot of Esprit sweatshirts waiting, like *tabulae rasae*, for the right pigeon to complete the fashion statement.

The Real Thing

Nothing gets my dander up faster than the phrase "real Chicago pizza." I mean, what is real? What is Chicago? What is pizza? (And what, for that matter, is dander?)

It's time somebody warned innocent Californians of the danger of this hoax. Otherwise they will continue to allow their taste buds to be molested by these counterfeits while assuming there's no need to go to Chicago for research. Why risk experiencing bad weather and being machine-gunned by some gangster if you can get the real thing here at home?

Many places in the area offer what purports to be "real Chicago pizza," but I've yet to find it. The worst offender is the so-called Uno's franchise chain—an insult to any of us who spent our youth waiting for hours on the windiest corner in the windy city for quintessential Chicago pizza. This pizza consisted of a fresh crust covered with herbs and tomatoes buried under enough mozzarella so that you could stretch the cheese from one end of Wrigley Field to the other without breaking the strand. This was brought to your table in a cast-iron skillet, sizzling hot, so that, unless you had a Studs Terkel–like Chicago chatterbox keeping you from it, you inevitably bit into it too soon and burned your mouth. This, then, is a major point. If you walk out with your oral mucosa unscathed—it's not the real thing.

What you get at these franchises instead of this lethal meltdown is a pile of stale mush on a cardboard crust in a fake iron skillet. It's not real. It's mozzarella Memorex.

I'm not saying you can't get good pizza in California. You can get wonderful gourmet pizza at Chez Panisse and all its imitators. This is brick-oven, top-ingredient, innovative combo pie—very tasty. For my money, it's one of the best additions yet to California cuisine. If you feel you must be more experimental, get a side order of nasturtiums.

You can also get real New York junk pizza. But California/ New York junk pizza will never recall Tony's on Broadway and 105th in Manhattan. I went to Tony's in the winter of 1963. Each time I walked into the place, Tony would say, "Hey, Natalie Wood, what you want?" I put on a quick twenty pounds falling for the Natalie Wood line. But had he said, "Hey, Anna Magnani," would I have kept coming back?

But what I am looking for when I hear "real Chicago pizza" is something that will transport me back in time, back to a certain graystone apartment house on a grimly real west side of Chicago in the winter of 1956. It was there in that sacred shrine, which I would memorialize with a plaque if I could, that I first took the mozzarella sacrament.

On that deadend street in the city without a heart, I was born-again Sicilian in the kitchen of my best friend Palma Zaccagnini. Even if the miracle of the oregano had never taken place, Palma was a great best friend. She looked and acted like Madonna, and she was tops in school at math. You could hang around with her, pick up the boyfriend discards, and learn exponentiation at the same time. She taught me the art of flirting, self-defense, eyelining, and the highly developed Catholic science of guilt elimination. She taught me to dance the Chicken to the Coasters' "Searchin' (Gonna Find Her)," although—let the record show—

she was a Pat Boone fan. But I never guessed that, through Palma, I would be exposed to the archetypal pizza pie.

When I visited her home the first time, I was surprised by how poor the Zaccagninis were. It wasn't just the three-room flat practically right on the new freeway. It wasn't just that she shared the bedroom with her big sisters, Mary Beth and Natalie, while her parents shared the living room with her little brothers, Peter and Paul. It was the dinner I had there that seemed particularly impoverished. They served canned Franco-American spaghetti and a loaf of Wonder Bread. (Years later I heard that Palma married the owner of a funeral home, and I pray it means she's come into some Mafia money and can afford fresh pasta.)

The second time I was over, the family, which was generous the way poor families frequently are, asked me to stay again. I was picky about my food and hesitated. But I loved how much they laughed together, so I decided to risk the Franco-American again. Unbeknown to me the grandmother from Sicily was staying there. (Where they put her, God only knows—on top of the fridge?) As we were seated around the kitchen table, a toothless white-haired woman, Our Lady of the Deep Pan, placed what appeared to me to be a piece of cake on my plate. It was thick, dry, slightly crunchy bread dough with a light tomatoey icing, graced with oregano, anointed with oil, and topped with a halo of mozzarella. Real Chicago pizza. *Marone,* it was good.

When Californians talk about "real Chicago pizza," they are obviously not thinking of Mama Zaccagnini. They are thinking of Mama Celeste. In order to come up with a reasonable facsimile, I was forced to learn to make pizza. Forced is perhaps too strong a word. Obviously, nobody put an Uzi to my head. Nevertheless, I think I have come up with a good alternative and am going to share. Before you finish the next ink-stained paragraph, you, my drooling reader, can begin your novitiate.

REAL CHICAGO PIZZA

1. Take one numbers runner and place in cement boots. Drive to Lake Michigan (optional step for those seeking surreal Chicago pizza).

2. Place checkered tablecloth and Chianti bottle with candle on table. Attach neon sign saying TONY's to outside window.

3. Place Julius LaRosa 78 on record player (alternative: Rosemary Clooney singing, "Come on-a My House").

4. Swear and gesture wildly. Begin dough.

THE DOUGH

1. (You can use any white bread dough, but here's mine.) Place one cup luke-hot water in a warmed bowl. Add one package or tablespoon yeast and dissolve. FADE TO SHELF.

2. Add one tablespoon sugar, one tablespoon oil, and a half-tablespoon salt. Mix.

3. Add flour to get right consistency. Right consistency is that of a baby's tushy. Should take three or so cups. Go by look and feel, not measurement (this is art, not life).

4. With oily hands and a floury board, knead.

5. Place kneaded tushy in well-oiled bowl in warm spot and let rise (about thirty minutes).

6. When risen, spank down, and with oily hands, spread in oily cast-iron skillet or any other receptacle you like. Cookie sheet is fine. Silver vase is weird. (If crust seems too big, break off some and shape into *La Pietà.*) Bake.

THE TOPPINGS

1. Easiest is to fingerpaint about a half can of tomato paste across the top, but you can also slave over homemade special

sauce for days. You can also just drizzle olive oil (we don't need virgin—this is the '80s) and add fresh tomato slices.

2. Add shitload of minced garlic and best oregano you can get. Crush oregano between your bare fingers. Add fresh basil if desired (or sweet william, for that matter).

3. Now add whatever your little heart desires: sautéed mushrooms, peppers, onions, zucchini, best sausages (which are not kosher no matter what you pay for them), or some other disgusting things some people like on their pizza. Kind of shove this stuff into the dough.

4. Top with fresh-grated parmesan and *lots* of sliced okay-quality (not top) mozzarella.

5. Let rise for doughier-than-thou effect or stick soon in really hot oven, up there in 475-degree city. Watch and pray. You may need to bake ten minutes before adding cheese. Take out when cheese starts to brown. IF dough is too soft, sue me (and cook without cheese first next time or let dough rise longer).

6. Dig in and burn roof of mouth.

That, give or take a few failures, and a few curses aimed my way, should take you there—Zaccagnini fields forever. If it doesn't work out and you see me walking down the street—walk on by. If you like it, you take my hand, kiss, and say, "Thank you, Godmother."

Turning Forty
(and other unmitigated disasters)

Et tu, J. C. Penney? Is it not enough that my bones know it, that my aching back feels it, that my feet show it? But then this letter: "Dear Ms. Kahn: On December 22 you'll be celebrating something special, your 42nd Birthday. If you act before that date you're eligible to apply for $20,000 in valuable life insurance protection . . . at a monthly premium that will never again be lower than it is right now!" (Ah, yes. Never again. Don't you think I'm aware that in this case we're talking about a linear progression? That what goes around won't be coming around— never again. But no, this is not enough for you. You must further beat my furrowed brow.) ". . . If you apply after your birthday, the insurance will still be available. But the rate increases on your birthday. Because life insurance premiums are based on age, the longer you wait to buy, the higher the rate. So, when December 22 rolls around and you turn 42, you move up to a higher rate. . . ."

You wanna take me higher? Well, it rolled around and I didn't go for it. But this was quite a birthday present, J.C. This was the unkindest cut of cake of them all. This was my reward for ten loyal years of socks and underwear? A reminder that we're dying,

Egypt, dying—as if I didn't know it in this year when Our Lord said I had to stop jogging. The spirit was willing but the foot was weak.

> *I grow old, I grow old.*
> *I shall wear my panty hose rolled.*

When are you going to write your turning-forty story, friends kept asking. It's only taken me about two years.

What a pathetic lot the baby-boomers are on this whole aging business, complaining about living to an age when people in many civilizations are dead. But we weren't supposed to grow up. I know I wasn't.

The fortieth birthday gives no shelter from the charge of middle age. Just the sight of it had me grasping at achievement like Harold Lloyd dangling from the arms of that giant clock. I guess I've succeeded. Strange men are calling and asking me to do lunch. But less certain than ever, I look back over my life, questioning how I came to be a nurse and a writer and an alleged grown-up, trying to find the point, the needle in the haystack of memories. There's a thrust to these reflections. It's a self-serving little needle, no doubt about it, but you've got to serve somebody.

My initial plan as a tormented twelve-year-old was to commit suicide on my twentieth birthday. Nothing melodramatic, just some birthday cake, a few Cokes, and a hundred aspirins. Twenty was old enough, I thought, because somehow I'd gotten it into my head that I was going to be a failure. I wrote in my diary that year: "If I live past twenty I'll be an alcoholic, a prostitute, or a drug addict." I'm not sure why I thought that then. I was doing well in sixth-grade math. But every spare chance I got, I rode the bus to Chicago's West Madison Street, my hometown's skid row. Then I'd get off and walk alone among the poor men lying in the street and the haggard, toothless whores. I felt I should look, rub my nose in it, so to speak.

I never really had a plan, an ambition, until quite recently.

When I hit twenty and it was clear that I was going to live, I began trying to be something when I grew up. Not really destined for alcoholism, junkiedom, or whoredom, I studied poetry in college and developed quite another self-image: Cassandra, the mad poetess. I identified with weird goodie-two-shoes Victorian heroines like Esther Summerson in *Bleak House*. "As a candle in the dark, so shines a good deed in a naughty world." I would renounce all worldly pleasures. Except sex. I would write thousands of beautiful poems and, like Emily Dickinson, they would find them in my underwear drawer, among the J. C. Penney's cotton briefs.

Twenty-one crept up on me and, still alive, I had to earn a living. The poetry market was as bust as it had been since Ovid. I would have to grow up. I would have to be something my mother called normal. Nobody else in the family had been obliged to do that. Why me?

I knew normal had something to do with driving a car, cooking your own food, and getting a job—all things I learned to do half my life ago, in my twenty-first year. As I recall, I thought I was damn slow to be learning these basics so late in life.

I went to work as a schoolteacher, inflicting poetry on horny teenagers. But, thank God, I was bailed out by the late '60s. It was like a reprieve from having to grow up.

During that "let's pretend" revolution, I began to grope around for some new role to play. As it happened, I'd found my way to the Free Clinic, a wonderful institution of the times, a virtual theater of medicine, and while there I remembered my ambition when I was four years old. I could be a nurse.

"You can't be a nurse," my mother had told me in the spring of 1948. "Remember you can't stand to look at blood." Of course. Not only couldn't I look at my knees when I cut them (which I did every day that year either running or skating or falling out of a tree), but I couldn't even walk past the butcher shop without closing my eyes. "Tell me when we're past it, Mommy," I would say, holding her hand and playing blind man.

We lived in a big old apartment with dark wooden walls. "Four bedrooms with double plumbing," my father would proudly announce. "In Moe Rosenberg's—the ward committeeman's— building." My sister and I slept in the bedroom off my parents' room. My grandmother, my Boubie, shared a room with Uncle Ben, the lawyer, the only educated brother. Uncle Leo slept in the little bedroom down the hall. Uncle Abe slept on the hide-a-bed in the sun parlor.

Every day, Chris Allen, beautiful, blond, a shiksa, a nurse, would come to take care of Boubie, who had diabetes and was confined to bed. Uncle Ben, my *objet d'Oedipus*, who yelled at me and looked like Humphrey Bogart, was in love with Chris Allen. I was in love with Uncle Ben. I wanted to be a nurse, but I sure didn't want to look at blood. When Boubie died that spring, Chris Allen stopped coming. I started kindergarten in the fall and said my ambition was "writer," which was odd since I still didn't know how to print.

My second-grade teacher, Miss Friedman, who kissed you if you were good, told us to write a poem about birds. I went home and wrote fifty of them and put them in a little book, which I illustrated with my big box of sixty-four Crayolas—the one with silver and magenta and burnt sienna. Miss Friedman kissed me twice and gave me a pass to go to every room and show my bird poems. I was a writer.

In the fifth grade, I had the reputedly nicest teacher in the school. "I got Sharkey!" I shouted when my report card came marked "Promoted to Miss Sharkey's room." Miss Sharkey hugged you if you were good. She taught us hip songs to sing, like the theme from *High Noon*.

One day while I was doing a math problem at the board, Miss Sharkey said, "Sit down, pest." I looked around and realized she was indeed addressing me. I'd made a mistake so bad, she thought I was joking. Miss Sharkey, the nicest teacher in the school, hated me. She called me "pest"! I, who tried so hard to do good deeds in a naughty world, was accused of deliberate pesthood. I looked down at my desk and watched the big teardrops plop down.

While at the Free Clinic, I learned to draw blood. Dr. Beach Conger taught us in the dining room of his house. First we stuck the needle in oranges and drew juice. Then we stuck them in each other. I remember standing there with a syringe full of Fran Dreier's blood, asking, "What should I do with it, Beach?" He reached into the china cabinet and took out a Limoges teacup. "Just dump it in here."

I realized that year I could become a nurse. It came to me one day when I walked down the street and the song "Suicide Is Painless," the theme song from M*A*S*H, started playing in my head. It was like the music of the spheres.

If the revolution happened, I'd be a war nurse like in an Ann Sheridan movie. If it didn't, I could just do good deeds. I went to nursing school and found Phyllis, my teacher and my friend. "It's okay if you're a fainter," she told me when she found me, ashen and sweaty, in the hospital utility room. I had been giving my first injection of a thick iron supplement into the buttocks of a pregnant woman. I pushed too fast and the syringe broke and the muddy orange fluid shot out all over the white hospital wall and my white nurse's dress. Phyllis held my hand and made me get back on the horse and give the shot again. "That's okay," the patient kept saying as I awkwardly gave her the needle. "I'm sorry," I told her three or four times.

That night I lay in bed and replayed the broken-syringe scene over and over in my head. How could I have done it? The orange mud kept hitting the white wall like fireworks.

I went through nursing school hating hospitals, in terror of making mistakes, constantly having to remind myself to breathe so I wouldn't become light-headed and pass out. One day on the neuro floor at Highland, the county hospital, a physician was giving us a patient's medical history. He stood over the bed of a smiling man and said, "He was driving along the freeway mind-ing his own business, when a drunk came along the wrong way doing eighty. Now he's paralyzed from the neck down." I forgot to inhale and fell to the floor.

Eventually I got into the macho of the hospital, the heroics of trying to do the most difficult good deeds, and requested a preceptorship in the intensive care unit. At the county hospital ICU, we saw an endless line of overdoses and suicide attempts. Suicide wasn't painless. It left people paralyzed, blind, brain dead.

Of course it was crazy of me, whose skills were verbal, whose clumsy little hands could barely perform fine motor tasks, to want to stick tubes into unconscious patients. One day another nurse taught me a trick: "Don't look at their faces as you push the catheter in." It *was* easier that way.

By the time I got out of nursing school, the revolution was over and I became a nurse practitioner doing routine office work: coughs, constipation, and contraception. I was impressed with how little interest medicine had in dealing with the unglamorous side of common pain and I began writing about it, first for patient handouts, then for magazines. "You're a good writer," someone said to me once about a story I'd done on strep throat. That was it for me. I heard the music of the spheres again: "Suicide is painless." I could be all that I could be.

In time, I felt I could do all right by my patients and I no longer lived in terror of making a mistake. Then I began reading about the "doctor glut." Nurse practitioners were supposed to have been the answer to the doctor shortage, so they didn't need us anymore. A doctor in New York sued a nurse practitioner for performing a Pap smear. The handwriting was on the wall. Just as teachers were unable to find work in the teacher glut of the previous decade, I had now educated myself into a second unemployable profession. Why not be a writer, then, that impractical thing I had always wished for but never felt I could really do?

Why not? Why not because: Writers are not normal; they're

egomaniacal, self-serving, pompous lunatics whose stock-in-trade is their own insanity. Yes, it seemed to be right up my alley.

An old lady on a bus once stood up and screamed at me, "Don't stare at me, girlie, you got searchin' eyes." What else is left when you've got searchin' eyes and you've learned to draw blood? Of course I would be a writer.

At first, I only published carefully researched, informational pieces for which I could earn about a hundred dollars for a month's work. Then I started to loosen up, and before long, my life was an open free newspaper.

I was still riddled with fear of making a mistake. I still wanted to do good deeds in a naughty world, but I began to publish glib pieces that some people said made them laugh. Other people got pissed, told me so on the street, questioned my moral worth in letters-to-the-editor columns. In an effort to avoid the box of "humorist," I also wrote serious stories that inevitably earned me a letter from a reader: "I fail to see the humor in this . . ."

I spend more and more time trying to fathom the rules of the writing profession. How does a good story about the hand that fed you differ from selling out your own mother? I made some rules for myself—like don't write about friends, you either do a saint's life or they hate you—then broke them. One I kept. I would never betray my patients, never share the unbelievable stories of pain, rape, naiveté, cruelty, and triumph that came to me in the nursing office.

Finally, I felt my life had some balance—the chance to do good as a nurse and be somewhat naughty in print. I had invested so much into not hurting people in the nursing office that I think I tried to deny the fact that I might possess the capacity to hurt with words. Over time, I received incredible support from the community who read my stories, support that egged me on, that worked against a long history of feeling worthless, that balanced the chip I carried on my shoulder from my childhood.

Then, one day, a patient wrote, "I was shocked by your story. You are a good nurse, but I will never come to your office again."

I tossed and turned that night and sent her a letter apologizing for offending her. Where I come from, if people get mad at you, you must have done something wrong.

That Christmas I wrote what I thought was a pretty funny story about Jesus's unfamous kid brother, Fred Christ. But when I saw it in the paper, I was shocked myself. Someone was going to hate me for this. I began to imagine that everyone who didn't tell me they liked it must hate me. But no letters came, so I started to relax, to take more chances. Two years later, in a coffee shop, the mother of one of my daughter's classmates said to me, "I love your stories. My husband and I argue about you all the time."

"What do you mean?" I asked.

"Well, he's a strict Catholic. He's never forgiven you for that story about Fred Christ."

I couldn't sleep again that night. Who needed this? I'd stop writing tomorrow, I vowed. But, like the junkie I once believed I would become, I woke up from a good dream the next morning and thought: *Just one more story and then I'll quit.*

My fortieth birthday was a horrible one. A book deal had fallen through. I couldn't believe how much this career, this "being a writer," meant to me. Why wasn't it enough that I was a mother, a jogger, a nurse? Could I actually be that unwieldy monster—Today's Ultimate Woman? Did I have to have it all?

Last year I set out to write a story on funny things that happened at the anti-apartheid demonstration. Sure enough, one day, several months after the story appeared, I came upon a man I like very much fixing his broken-down car. He customarily greets me with a hug. This time, he looked up from his engine and shouted, "You're lost. You're a fascist. How can you make fun of the ragtag people?"

Had I really done that? I didn't think so. Once again I started slipping and sliding, tossing and turning all night long, thinking about what he had said. I wrote him a note apologizing the next day. I talked about it to other friends, other writers. "You're too thin-skinned," someone said. I wondered if he could stand to look at blood.

The secret to giving a good injection is to summon up your aggression and shoot the needle through the skin like a spear. Any hesitation, any wavering, any indirection, will cause pain. Would it were so with words.

Recently I've been hearing from dissatisfied customers. First the lady at the local bookstore—one of those small local bookstores that make it possible for small local authors to sell books—asked me why I'd written a negative remark about the shopping center where she works. "Don't you know how hard we merchants are struggling to make a living?"

No sooner had the dark circles formed under my eyes over that one than a relative, one of the few I've got alive, one of the few I've ever liked, let it be known how offended she was by a story in my book which implied a negative view of a member of her family. I cried over that and sweated it out through the whole Christmas season, not hearing from her for the first time.

Probably the question I've been asked the most in the past three months is, "How does it feel to be a success?"—because I published a book, a dream come true. First of all, I tell them, I'm still hoping to earn a living as a writer—maybe someday, if I'm lucky, make as much as a nurse. And while recognition is nice, there are times I want to crawl back into my hole and forget it. Increasingly, I find myself motivated not by a desire to succeed but by petty emotions—anger over deprivations that ended twenty-five years ago, the desire for revenge on those who rejected me, wanting to create a feeling of regret in certain editors who treated me like some toothless hag of a skid-row whore. Someone wrote a story about me in a local paper asking, Will success spoil her? The real question I keep asking myself is, Did forty-one years of failure spoil me? Make me just a wee bit ruthless?

Don't let it *get* to you, people say. Everything *gets* to me. How did other grown-ups learn to be so tough? I wish they would teach me not to care. Maybe then I'd get some sleep. Why can't I just respond like Fellini did when he was pursued by the communist youths yelling, "Federico, Federico, why do you show whores and lowlife? Why not show something uplifting?" "I may be wrong," he said, "but I believe you do what you can."

Once I tried to run up Claremont Canyon, the steepest, longest jog in town. Couldn't do it. Had to stop and walk. Eventually I hitched a ride home. After I learned my limits, jogging became boring, although I slogged along for another five years until my foot hurt so much that I could hardly walk without pain. Then, this year—the year that J. C. Penney reminded me to buy now, death's a-comin'—I couldn't run anymore.

Last week D. came into the office looking smashing—that's the word, smashing. "You look terrific," I told her.

"Well, the last time I was here was my thirtieth birthday and you said, 'Thirty's your last chance to be a pretty girl.'"

Later in the week, N. came in and said, "I feel terrible. I'm turning forty. I didn't mind thirty. But this is *physical.*"

"I know," I told her. "We were feminists, we weren't supposed to care. When I turned forty, I remembered I was supposed to be a writer when I grew up. Well, this is it. I am grown up. It's either write or get off the pot."

What's Love Got to Do with It?

I'm like a virgin, which is to say I'm married. Actually, I'm what is known in the trade as very married. Having stayed with my "first husband" (my high school sweetheart) for nearly twenty years, I have seen attitudes toward marriage change from the prevailing positive currents of 1966 (the year we tied the knot) to the increasingly antimarriage eras of the late '60s and '70s and now full circle to the mating panic of the '80s.

I have noticed that people who remained married through those turbulent times appear relatively innocent about love. Not having participated in either the wild sexual experimentation or the profound disillusionment that marked the anything-goes era, my husband and I now seem almost virginal compared to the legions of love-scarred adults our age.

Frankly, I never approached marriage with a this-is-forever, holy, sacred vows attitude. In fact, I remember thinking as I approached the rabbi in the decidedly unromantic setting of Chicago's Loop Synagogue. "What the hell? If it doesn't work out, we can always get divorced."

The husband-to-be was also having some unsettling thoughts about the whole arrangement: he was sweating like a pig. As we were told to join hands, a huge drop of sweat fell on the simple gold band, purchased earlier from a cigar-smoking uncle who let us "have it" for $7.95. I shot my beloved one of those look-buddy-nobody's-holding-a-gun-to-your-goddamn-head glances.

Diamonds are forever but it's the simple gold band that still rests on third finger, left hand. The finger never turned green although the Florentine pattern wore off a decade ago. I suspect that those people who approached the rabbi (or holy person of their choice) with "this will be perfect, now I'll be happy forever" hocked the diamond a long time ago—shortly after the divorce settlement.

Upon completing the marriage ceremony, the rabbi boasted that he had stop-watched the proceedings, "start to finish," at four and a half minutes. Following this, about a hundred relatives and the few friends who could make the journey from our colleges back East and our new home in California were invited to "share our joy" at a reception held in my sister's suburban backyard.

The relatives scarfed up the repast as if they were still starving in Europe. We, the bride and groom, never even got a shot at the crab mousse. On an empty stomach, we drank glass after glass of champagne and merrily kissed Aunt Esther and Uncle Sol, whom we would never see again (I could hardly even focus on them that bubbly afternoon). As soon as it was possible to get away, we went out for hamburgers with four friends who had also graduated from college the year before. While seated at the suburban sandwich shop, our friend Dobby pulled his wife's bra out of his coat pocket. We all giggled. We were twenty-two years old.

The wedding was about as romantic as an Abbott and Costello movie or the proposal itself. Instead of kneeling with a little velvet box in his hand, my future husband came up to me one day and said, "I was reading an article in *Time* magazine about marriages that last."

"Yeah?" I said, wondering why he was telling me this.

"It said that if high school sweethearts get married, they have a statistically more significant chance of staying married than non high school sweethearts."

"Yeah?" I responded, not quite sure if he was saying what I thought he was saying.

"Well," he said after a significant pause, "I kind of figured: That's us."

So we approached the marriage ritual with a statistical edge and a desire for brevity. I think we both felt the marriage was for our mothers. What *we* really wanted was to live together, to sleep together, to not have to say good-bye on Sunday night.

During that year before we got married, Sunday night on the F bus was the cruelest time. I would leave him at his little apartment in Berkeley, where we happily shared a single bed, where we delighted in my first culinary conquest—Lawry's spaghetti sauce—where we fumbled our way through the newly developed contraceptive technologies. When I waved good-bye from the bus and began the long and painful ride back to my small apartment in San Francisco, I'd feel disconnected. The East Bay Terminal loomed like some lonely Edward Hopper painting. As I rode the M car back to the Ingleside district, the last thing on my mind was a wedding ceremony, dish patterns, joint IRAs, two-career couples, or children. All I cared about, baby, was *being with you*.

Had we waited a year or two, we probably wouldn't have gotten married. By then, living together was becoming the norm. I think our mothers could have handled it without constant tearful long-distance calls about our shame and their humiliation. Besides, by 1969 we were in full rebellion against everything they held sacred. Marriage was becoming an embarrassment, something to conceal from our friends in their communes, something to hide when the speaker at the rally shouted, "Bomb the nuclear family," something to hope the comrades in my women's group never confronted me with.

Sometime around 1970, during the great bourgeois purge, I threw out the wedding album. I couldn't bear to look at myself in that little Jackie Kennedy dress with my sprayed hair and my rehearsed dark lipstick smile. I think my husband was just as glad to eliminate the evidence linking him to tie wearing, face shaving, and incredibly short hair. This was also probably when we sold the furniture at a garage sale and gave away the matching mono-grammed glasses.

During the '70s, divorce rates soared. The Bay Area's was among the highest in the nation. Our acquaintances split apart and, since the settlement never included who got the friends, we'd lose touch with both members of the couple. My mother died and his father died, and we held on to each other like two in a lifeboat.

We had children and one day, one of our daughters came back from a friend's house and asked, "Where do I live? My mom's house or my dad's house?"

Then, around two or three years ago, we started getting wedding invitations again. Frequently, the bride would walk down the aisle in the parlor of the bed-and-breakfast inn carrying her newborn baby. And people would ask us for our secret. How did we stay together? With all the incredible renewed interest in family life and the longing to return to the days of Lake Wobegon, people wanted to know how we had maintained what sometimes seemed like the only living family near San Francisco Bay. And frankly, I often do wonder how we have made it together full circle, back to the two-career, parenting couple, my-IRA-or-yours world of the '80s.

Whenever I am asked for our secret, I always think of a day when we were seniors in high school. At that time I had no vision of the future, no plan for myself, just immediate needs and long-ing. And there was this boy. I liked him very much—more than I cared to admit. We'd always run into each other between fourth and fifth periods and we'd talk on the way to English class. "Whaddaya think of Eustacia Vye?" "She's a dip." Stuff like that.

On this day, I hid. Was it an accident that we met? I wanted to know if these meetings were more than casual for him too. Then

I peered at him, hanging out by his locker, looking down the hall for me, waiting and watching until after the bell rang.

The wedding was a comedy (although I wish I still had the album). But this was serious. This was when I knew that the love that's got to do with it was there.

"SELF-ADMITTED SMART-ASS, WICKED, SMUTTY, IRREV-ERENT TO A FAULT, AND VERY FUNNY."

— *Vogue*

WHAT THEY'RE SAYING ABOUT

Alice Kahn

HER COLUMN AND HER BOOKS

"HER OBSERVATIONS OF CONTEMPORARY LIFE CAN BE ACUTE, HER REFLECTIONS ON THE PAST POIGNANT... SHE CONNECTS FIRMLY WITH HER READERS' FEARS, AFFECTIONS AND MEMORIES."

— *Philadelphia Inquirer*

"SHE'S ONE OF THE HOTTEST THINGS TO HIT NON-FICTION WRITING SINCE TOM WOLFE DICED NEW JOURNALISM WITH OLD...SHARP OBSERVATIONS, SLANGY AUTHORITY, AND GOOD REPORTORIAL IN-STINCTS."

— *The Kansas City Star*

"*MULTIPLE SARCASM*...[IS] THE FUNNIEST STUFF BE-TWEEN COVERS. I'D HAPPILY STEAL JUST ABOUT ALL OF IT IF I COULD."

— *Garrison Keillor*

"A REAL TREAT. INCISIVE AND WITTY...A FRESH EYE AND ORIGINAL PEN...SHE CAN BE OUTRAGEOUS."

— *MS. Magazine*

"A SELF-DESCRIBED SIT-DOWN COMIC...FOR THOSE WHO WOULD LIKE TO LAUGH THEIR UPWARDLY MO-BILE HEADS OFF."

— *The Washington Post Book World*

A DELL TRADE PAPERBACK
Dell Publishing Co., Inc.

Cover design © 1988 by
Andrew M. Newman
Cover photo © 1988 by
Chris Stewart/San Francisco Chronicle

50795

9 780440 501572

N 0-440-50157-1>>795